Sugar Pie & Jelly Roll

Also by
Robbin Gourley

Cakewalk

Sugar Pie Jelly & Roll

Sweets from a Southern Kitchen

written and illustrated by

Robbin Gourley

ALGONQUIN BOOKS OF CHAPEL HILL

2000

Published by
Algonquin Books of Chapel Hill
Post Office Box 2225
Chapel Hill, North Carolina 27515-2225

a division of
Workman Publishing
708 Broadway
New York, New York 10003

Printed in China.
Published simultaneously in Canada
    by Thomas Allen & Son Limited.
Design by Anne Winslow.

Library of Congress Cataloging–in–Publication Data
Gourley, Robbin.
    Sugar pie & jelly roll: sweets from a southern kitchen / written and illustrated by
    Robbin Gourley.
        p. cm.
    Includes index.
    ISBN 1-56512-275
    1. Desserts. 2. Cookery, American—Southern style. I. Title.
    TX773 .G663 2000
    641.8'6—dc21   00-055827

10 9 8 7 6 5 4 3 2 1
First Edition

To Elouise and Norman

Contents

viii Baking Tips
  x Acknowledgments
 xi Introduction

1 PIES, CRISPS & CRUMBLES

Pie Shell
Buttermilk Pie
Chess Pie
Chocolate Chess Pie
Muzz's Lemon Chess Pie
Classic Southern Pecan Pie
Peace Pie
Bramble Crumble
Apple Crisp
Fried Fruit Pies
Coconut Custard Pie
Pumpkin Chiffon Pie
Shoofly Pie
Lemon Meringue Pie
Moon Pie

29 PUDDINGS & CUSTARDS

Mom's Cherry Pudding
Wild Persimmon Pudding
Banana Pudding
Raspberry Summer Pudding
November Pudding
Apricot Bread Pudding
Chocolate Pudding
Kay Bennett's Deep-Dish
   Sweet Potato Pudding
Pears in Nightshirts

47 CANDY

Peanut Brittle
Caramels
Divinity
Mother's Fudge
Chocolate-Covered Peanut
   Butter Bonbons
Candied Fruit Peels Dipped
   in Chocolate
Pralines
Pulled Mints
Simple Butter Mints
Miss Trixie's Candied Popcorn
Opera Creams

65 COOKIES & BARS

Chess Chewies
Orange Blossoms
Pam's Frosty Date Balls
Gumdrop Cookies
Meringue Surprises
Pecan Drops
Libby Robbins's Scotchies
Mrs. Whitmore's Cookies
Lemon Kisses

79 FAVORITE CAKES

Fig Cake
Jelly Roll
Burnt-Sugar Cake with Burnt-
    Sugar Frosting
Christmas Orange Cake
Sugar-Crust Pound Cake with
    Sherry Sauce
Warm Chocolate Cake
Pam's Persimmon-Apple Cake
Cream Puffs

101 CHILLED & SPIRITED DESSERTS

Peach Ice Cream
Snow Cream
Frozen Fruit Compote
Ambrosia
Wine Jelly
Poached Peaches with Whole
    Peppercorns
Figs in Spiced Wine
Syllabub

115 EMBELLISHMENTS

Raspberry Sauce
Bourbon Sauce
Hot Fudge Sauce
Real Whipped Cream
Aunt Leecie's Custard Sauce
Norman's Nog

121 Index

Baking Tips

Have all ingredients at room temperature (unless otherwise indicated). Softened butter means butter at room temperature. You can hasten softening by placing butter in the microwave for forty-five seconds on low power. Allow to sit for an additional two minutes. Bring eggs to room temperature quickly by setting them in a bowl of warm water for several minutes.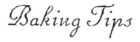

Always use unsalted butter unless otherwise specified.

Always use large eggs.

Because of salmonella contamination, licking the bowl or spoon of batter containing raw eggs is not a good idea.

Use the purest, freshest ingredients to insure intense flavors. Use real extracts instead of imitations.

The cooler the temperature of the kitchen, the easier it is to work pie pastry and candies. Make pastry before you preheat the oven.

When using a double boiler, do not let the boiling water touch the bottom of the top bowl or the mixture could burn.

Grease pans with unsalted butter or shortening—never with oil.

Always preheat the oven for at least 20 minutes.

Test your oven for accuracy. Use reputable oven thermometers, preferably more than one.

Place your pie on the bottom shelf of a three-rung oven, or the second from the bottom of a four-rung oven, the most evenly heated spot in the oven.

Don't pull your pie out of the oven until it is just nut-brown (unless otherwise specified in the recipe).

You can protect a pie edge from overbrowning by using a pie-edge protector cut from aluminum foil. Cut foil into a 12-inch square. Trace the outline of the bottom of a 9-inch pie pan (or 8-inch pan, if that's the size you are using) onto the foil. Cut along the outline to remove the circle in the center of the foil. Lay the square on top of the pie, covering the edges and crimping slightly to hold the foil in place. This works very well and will help prevent underbaked pies.

When the recipe calls for a 9-inch pie shell, be sure to use the correct size. In other words, don't put the filling for a 9-inch pie into an 8-inch shell, or the pie will overflow while baking.

In my opinion, glass baking dishes produce the most consistent and best results. Glass conducts heat evenly and allows you to see when you have a beautifully browned and dry crust bottom.

Place fruit pies on rimmed cooking sheets while baking to prevent spills and to protect oven racks.

Cakes and baked puddings are done when they begin to pull away from the sides of the pan or when a knife inserted in the middle comes out clean.

Use cake flour when called for in recipes. Cake flour is made of soft wheat and is sifted in the milling process; all-purpose flour is made from a blend of hard and soft wheat. Cake flour produces a crumblier texture and a higher volume cake; all-purpose flour results in a denser, sturdier texture. You may substitute 1 cup minus 2 tablespoons sifted all-purpose flour for 1 cup cake flour. Or, if the recipe calls for 1 cup all-purpose flour, you can use 1⅛ cup cake flour.

ACKNOWLEDGMENTS

Acknowledging the countless people who have had an influence on this book would be fruitless, a difficult notion for a dessert cookbook. Beyond my immediate family, there are more mothers, grandmothers, sisters, aunts and great-aunts, cousins, and friends' kin from Missouri, Arkansas, Georgia, Virginia, North and South Carolina whose recipes are included as originally conceived or with slight variations. You know who you are.

I am indebted to Elisabeth Scharlatt for everything—her vision, her enthusiasm for books, and her tireless desire to make good things happen. Thanks to Kathy Pories for her strong editorial pen and to Anne Winslow, art director extraordinaire.

To Susan Overman, Southern compatriot and guide, mentor in the kitchen, this effort owes so much to you. Susan, your collaboration has made this a stronger book.

Thanks to an ever brilliant and lovable team at Algonquin: Dana Stamey, Amy Hayworth, Antonia Fusco, and Andra Olenik.

At age five, I received a diminutive tin refrigerator,
a tiny electric stove that really baked, and miniature baking
sheets and muffin tins from Santa Claus. Packaged mixes that
needed only water and a stir were
arranged beside my small kitchen.
My obsession with desserts began that
Southern Christmas day, and I had not
a particle of doubt about it.

Introduction

OUTHERNERS HAVE MADE SUGAR their business
since Colonial times. But that only partially explains
why my relatives consider themselves experts when it
comes to dessert. Our ancestors had big farm kitchens, stations for
more than one cook or baker, and many hungry mouths to feed.
Dessert had always been an essential part of every meal; a pleasur-
able awakening for the palate after a heartening repast. Dessert
satisfied the soul after bolstering the body and helped to supply the
needed calories to carry on the hard work in the fields. It even made
the afternoon's work look brighter.

In the land of Dixie, personalities can be downright sugary. The favorite nickname in my family is "sug," but others include "honey," "sweet pea," "toots" (pronounced tuutz), and "cookie." I like to think that words are drawled just because they sound sweeter. And in my family, a person's attachment to a certain sweet is a part of them like the way they wear their hat or overuse their favorite expression. My grandfather always had a hankering for cherry pudding; my mother adores all things chocolate. My sister Pam prefers lemon anything, while for my father, it's maple pecan. Uncle L.A., the beekeeper, loves persimmon pudding, and Aunt Sue always has a batch of nut candy on hand.

Where I come from, dessert is not only served after dinner. It can be breakfast, lunch, or dinner. I remember at one opulent family feast Aunt Bett pronouncing, "Tonight, I'm having dessert first." And on a long-ago snowy December morning, after rising at daybreak and trudging through the woods to find the perfect Christmas tree and carrying it back home, my Dad and I helped ourselves to a very large slice of homemade Christmas Orange Cake for breakfast. We were happy all day.

I have seen desserts similar to my Southern favorites in the cases of fancy bakeries in New York. These smart marketers know that a good idea never grows old, it just needs repackaging. Their presentations are lavish: a round chocolate torte embellished with a fleur-de-lis of confectioners' sugar looks just like my warm chocolate cake dusted with sugar through a child's handmade snowflake pattern. The tea cakes wrapped in transparent paper and tied with hemp in Monsieur Bouley's patisserie are the same as my Lemon Kisses wrapped and tied with a handsome ribbon snipped from my kitchen drawer. I challenge even Mr. DeLuca to compare Muzz's Lemon Chess Pie to his Tarte Citron!

These tried and improved-upon recipes are from the honorable tradition of Southern baking, which borrows liberally from African, English, and French cookery. My hope is that these desserts will make happy memories in some other lives as well. A thoughtfully prepared and beautifully presented dessert brings a group together like bees to honey.

Sugar Pie & Jelly Roll

Pies, Crisps & Crumbles

Voodoo

A slice of buttermilk pie was placed before me. The top glistened with a veneer of caramelized sugar. Mother ordered her favorite chocolate chess pie, something she'd been doing at the café at Belk for at least thirty years. As soon as she raised her fork, I cut into my pie gingerly.

"So, Mom," I asked, "what's going on with Mary?"

The pie tasted sweet, yet tangy. The crust was perfect, dry and flaky, holding its own against the light, but creamy, buttermilk.

"Well, all I know is she has been having an affair for years and in my book that's just asking for something terrible to happen."

I must have been thinking too hard about the pie. I dropped my fork. It clattered to the floor.

"Don't pick it up!" Mom hissed, eyes level over her teacup.

I heeded her warning. A black cat in her path would make her cross herself seven times. A dropped fork was just as mortifying and could produce as many years of bad luck as breaking a mirror.

I took a sip of coffee and a long look at Mom, still trim and beautiful. And, once again, because I let the waiter pick up the fork, we, unlike Mary, were spared some grave misfortune.

PIE SHELL

*This is the classic American pie shell, not to be confused
with French tart pastry. Vegetable shortening or lard insures
a very flaky crust; however, it is much more delicate than
crust made with butter and more frustrating to handle. But
persevere—crusts take only practice, determination, and a
dash of confidence. Be sure your shortening is very cold.
Add the water with a very light hand, and don't be tempted
to add too much; the dough may come together better, but it
will be hard and tough once baked. Roll out with light
strokes from the center, preferably on a cool surface.*

ONE 8-OR 9-INCH PIE SHELL

(Double the recipe for a double crust.)

1¼ cups all-purpose flour
½ teaspoon salt
⅓ cup chilled shortening
    (vegetable shortening or butter or a combination)
3 to 4 tablespoons ice water

In a mixing bowl, sift flour and salt together. Cut in
shortening with a pastry blender, two knives, or with
your fingers for about a minute until pieces resemble
small peas. Sprinkle 1 tablespoon of the cold water
over part of the mixture and gently toss with a
fork. Push to the side of the bowl. Repeat until all
flour is moistened. Do not overwork mixture or crust
will be tough.

Using your hands, quickly form dough into a ball. If it
is a double crust, divide into 2 balls. Wrap in plastic
and refrigerate for 30 minutes (or up to 3 days). The
dough can be frozen for later use.

Sugar Pie

Gather scraps of leftover dough into a ball, roll out into a small circle, and place on an ungreased cookie sheet or pie pan. Score into four sections, sprinkle with sugar and cinnamon, and bake in 350°F oven for 5 to 10 minutes, watching carefully until it bakes to a lovely light brown. Eat it sitting on the back steps because it crumbles easily and makes a mess. Eat it fast—everyone will want some. Once when my Uncle Tom was visiting, he made a batch of piecrust and rolled the whole thing out into a big sugar pie. He was homesick.

Sprinkle work surface lightly with flour. Flatten dough into a disk with hands. Roll out the dough from the center to the edge, into a circle slightly larger than 8 or 9 inches and ease gently into pie pan without stretching dough. (You can wrap the dough around the rolling pin and unroll into the pie pan.) Trim excess dough from edge, then turn under and crimp, flute, or scallop the edges. Bake as directed in individual recipes.

Blind Baking

Blind baking is completely prebaking a pie shell—a relatively new development. When I was growing up, nobody in my family really seemed to mind a less-than-crisp bottom crust, and some even seemed to prefer it soggy. However, starting the baking in a hot oven assures a flakier, crisper crust, which I've come to favor.

To blind bake, preheat oven to 425°F. Press crust firmly, but without stretching, into the pie pan. Refrigerate the crust for 20 minutes. When ready to bake, prick the crust all over with a fork, cover with a sheet of heavy duty foil—buttered lightly on the side that touches the crust—and fill the bottom with rice or dried beans (which can be kept and reused again as pie weights) or with another pie pan. Bake the crust for 12 minutes; remove from oven. Reduce heat to 350°F, and remove weights and foil. Bake another 10 to 15 minutes until light brown. Cool.

BUTTERMILK PIE

An old, old classic, predating the Civil War. Tangy and refreshing, this is a stunningly simple dessert best served with seasonal berries.

8 SERVINGS

½ cup butter, melted
3 eggs, beaten
1 cup buttermilk
1 teaspoon vanilla
1 cup sugar
2 tablespoons all-purpose flour
¼ teaspoon salt
One 9-inch blind-baked pie shell

Preheat oven to 325°F.

Mix together butter, eggs, buttermilk, and vanilla. Add sugar, flour, and salt and mix well. Pour into a 9-inch blind-baked pie shell. Bake until the pie is set but slightly jiggly in the center, about 25 minutes. Serve with fresh, seasonal berries.

Chess Pie

The expression "easy as pie" must have something to do with chess pies. They never fail, always please a crowd, and can be made in a skinny minute. I've even mixed one up to serve for dessert while my husband cleared the dinner plates.

8 SERVINGS

½ cup butter
1¼ cups sugar
2 tablespoons yellow
    cornmeal
3 eggs, slightly beaten
1 teaspoon vanilla
One 9-inch unbaked pie shell

Preheat oven to 375°F.

Cream butter, sugar, and cornmeal in a large bowl. Add eggs and vanilla and beat well. Pour into pie shell. Bake in oven for 15 minutes. Lower heat to 350°F and bake for another 20 minutes. Serve hot or cold.

Note: The problem with chess pies is that despite the sublime pleasure they deliver, they are ugly as sin. (So don't present them as le grande finale.) Slice the pieces before you bring them to the table, and serve them on a beautiful dessert plate with a garnish: a sprig of thyme, tiny mint leaves or lavender flowers (fresh or dried), a poof of whipped cream, or a curl of orange or a lemon peel.

"Jus' pie, Honey!"

Someone once told me that chess pies got their name when a cook was asked what she was baking and she replied, "Jus' pie, Honey!" It's a good story, very Southern, like the pie itself—and probably not true. James Beard thought that chess pie had come from England, even though it's not standard fare there anymore. Jefferson Davis pies, transparent pies, and chess pies are all part of the same family—made with a mixture of eggs, butter, and sugar that sets to a firm, transparent custard.

CHOCOLATE CHESS PIE

Redolent of winter gatherings. When more than one kind of dessert is offered, this pie pleases the chocolate lovers.

8 SERVINGS

½ cup butter
Two 1-ounce squares unsweetened chocolate
1 cup firmly packed brown sugar
½ cup sugar
2 eggs, slightly beaten
1 teaspoon all-purpose flour
1 tablespoon milk
1 teaspoon vanilla
One 9-inch unbaked pie shell

Preheat oven to 325°F.

Melt butter and chocolate in small saucepan over low heat. In a medium bowl, combine sugars, eggs, flour, milk, and vanilla, stirring well. Gradually add chocolate mixture, stirring constantly. Pour into pie shell and bake for 40 to 45 minutes. Let cool slightly before eating, or serve warm with whipped cream or Aunt Leecie's Custard Sauce (p.119) if you must gild the lily.

Carrying a Torch

Propane welding torches are excellent for caramelizing sugar toppings, especially since the oven's broiler can produce uneven results. Caramelizing provides a custard pie with a lovely golden top that cracks when it is cut with a fork. A propane torch has a localized and powerful flame that is hot enough to caramelize sugar perfectly. With practice, torches are really safe to use.

To caramelize, sprinkle the top of the dessert with a thin, even layer of granulated sugar. Turn the torch on low and light with a match with the nozzle pointing away from you. The flame should be steady and not sputter. Raise the flame to high and direct it toward the dessert, about three to four inches from the top. Sweep the flame side to side in a slow, even motion, avoiding the pastry crust so as not to brown it further. The sugar will start to brown as you sweep across, but if the sugar begins to bubble and burn or turn dark brown or black, blow it out to cool it off and stop the burning.

Caramelized sugar loses its crunchiness after thirty minutes, so it's best to torch the dessert right before serving.

Butane chef's torches are available at kitchenware specialty stores and cost from thirty to forty dollars. I use my husband's welding torch with a small tank of propane, which can be purchased at the local hardware store for much less. Read the manufacturer's instructions carefully before starting, and practice first.

Muzz's Lemon Chess Pie

Whereupon simplicity is perfected.

8 SERVINGS

1 cup sugar
1 tablespoon all-purpose flour
1 tablespoon cornmeal
4 eggs, beaten
4 tablespoons melted butter
¼ cup milk
¼ cup fresh lemon juice
1 teaspoon grated lemon peel
1 teaspoon vanilla
2 teaspoons granulated sugar for caramelizing
One 9-inch unbaked pie shell

Partially bake pie shell for 5 minutes at 450°F. Remove the shell and cool. Reduce oven to 350°F.

Mix the sugar with the flour and cornmeal in a large bowl. Add in the eggs and beat by hand until the mixture is light and lemon-colored. Add the butter, milk, lemon juice, lemon zest, and vanilla and mix well. Pour into partially baked pie shell. Bake for 30 minutes until firm. Chill in the refrigerator for 1 hour.

To serve, preheat broiler. Sprinkle a layer of granulated sugar over the pie, covering the surface with sugar, and set the pan in a slightly larger pan of ice to prevent the custard from heating up. Place the pan under the broiler until the sugar is caramelized. (Or use a torch to caramelize the sugar.) Serve immediately.

Libidinous Kerfuffle

A longtime beau of mine could outfox, outrun, and outeat any man in Wake County. Lanky, handsome, and skinny as a bean, he consumed more at one sitting than any other man I have ever known. It was his habit (passed along to him by his father) to lie down on the Persian carpet after a meal with a cup of tea balanced on his belly. He claimed not to be able to move from the innumerable helpings he consumed.

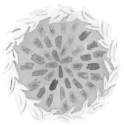

At the beginning, it was difficult for me to compete with his love for the guitar and the company of his rogue friends, but soon I learned to trick him into spending an afternoon with me. Pecan pie was the bait. He ate the entire thing. It took about three hours for the pie to disappear, and after he had recovered, I had his rather dazed, but undivided attention.

Classic Southern Pecan Pie

A perfect way to remind everyone of the coziness of autumn and winter.

8 SERVINGS

3 eggs
⅔ cup brown sugar
⅓ cup butter, melted
¼ teaspoon salt
1 cup dark corn syrup
1 teaspoon vanilla
1 cup finely chopped pecans or pecan halves
One 9-inch unbaked pie shell

Preheat oven to 375°F.

In a mixing bowl, beat together eggs and sugar. Add butter, salt, and corn syrup. Mix in pecan halves. Pour into the pie shell. Bake until set and nicely browned, about 40 to 50 minutes. Serve slightly warm with a dollop of whipped cream.

Peace Pie

For a sweet, sparkly top crust, spread a light coat of water with a pastry brush onto the top of the pastry before baking your pie. Sprinkle with brown or turbinado sugar and bake.

This versatile recipe will work with fresh berries as well. Substitute 5½ cups of another seasonal fruit like cherries or blackberries and toss in a teaspoon of freshly grated ginger for more punch.

A typographical error in a recipe from my mother resulted in this wonderfully named pie. It was supposed to be Peach Pie. Serve warm with a dollop of whipped cream and a sprinkling of lavender flowers for a ravishing finish.

8 SERVINGS

Pastry for double-crust pie
7 large peaches
1¼ cups sugar
1 teaspoon lemon juice
6 tablespoons butter, cut into pieces

Preheat oven to 450°F.

Prepare a double piecrust (p.3). Roll out and line an 8 × 8 × 2-inch glass baking dish with half of the dough. Sprinkle 2 tablespoons of sugar over the pastry. Roll out the remaining dough and cut into strips for a lattice top. Wrap the dish and the strips in plastic and refrigerate until you are ready to assemble the pie.

Peel, pit, and slice the peaches. Mix with the sugar and spread evenly in the pastry-lined dish. Sprinkle the lemon juice over the peaches. Dot with pats of butter. Weave the lattice top, moisten the rim with cold water, and seal the edges.

Bake the pie in the oven for 10 minutes at 450°F, then lower the heat to 425°F for another 35 minutes. Remove from the oven and let the pie rest for 30 minutes. Serve warm with your favorite cream topping.

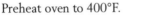

BRAMBLE CRUMBLE

Filling:

4 cups fresh blackberries,
gently washed and
drained
4 to 6 tablespoons sugar

Crumble:

½ cup almonds
½ cup all-purpose flour
⅓ cup sugar
¼ cup butter,
softened

Preheat oven to 400°F.

Arrange the berries in a buttered 8 × 8 × 2-inch glass baking dish. Sprinkle the sugar over them. Roast the almonds on a cookie sheet in the oven for 15 minutes, stirring and turning every 3 minutes or so until the nut has a golden center when broken open. Let cool, and then grind to a mealy texture in a food processor.

To make the crumble, mix flour, sugar, and ground almonds in a small bowl. Cut in the butter with two knives or a pastry blender until it's a crumbly consistency. Sprinkle the crumble evenly over the berries.

Bake at 400°F for 20 minutes, then lower the heat to 350°F and bake for 20 more minutes or until the top is nicely browned. Serve warm with your favorite topping: whipped cream, ice cream, or heavy cream.

Note: Other berries may be used, as well as pears or peaches.

Blackberry brambles

are notorious for thorns. The berries you get from them feel like prizes, so it seems right to name a pie after the fight in the bramble. A kind of victory for the people, so to speak.

APPLE CRISP

The answer to the perfect apple crisp question.

4 TO 6 SERVINGS

3 to 4 Granny Smith apples (or tart
   apples of your choice)
1¼ cups sugar
⅓ cup butter, divided
¼ cup orange juice
Dash of salt
½ teaspoon cinnamon
¼ teaspoon nutmeg
¾ cup sifted all-purpose
   flour

Crisps, Crunches, & Crumbles

These simple and satisfying desserts all appear to have a common origin in the old European practice of using stale bread crumbs to vary the texture of baked fruit. Now we do this with an assortment of additions: nuts, oats, and flour— or a combination of them.

Preheat oven to 375°F.

Peel, core, and chop the apples and mix with 1 cup of the sugar in a small bowl. Pile them into an 8 × 8-inch pan greased with 1 tablespoon of the butter. Pour the orange juice over the apples. In a small bowl, sift the salt, spices, flour, and remaining sugar together. Cut the rest of the butter into the flour mixture with two knives until it forms a small pea texture. Sprinkle the mixture over top of the apples.

Bake 45 to 50 minutes. Serve warm with a drift of whipped cream or a scoop of vanilla ice cream.

Note: For a little something naughty, substitute applejack brandy for the orange juice.

Fig Cake

The simple task of gathering the ingredients is all the finesse one needs for this sturdy and satisfying cake. It's very toothsome served warm with a touch of whipped cream.

10 TO 12 SERVINGS

2 cups all-purpose flour
1 teaspoon cinnamon
1 teaspoon nutmeg
1 teaspoon allspice
1 teaspoon baking soda
½ teaspoon salt
1 cup vegetable oil
1½ cups sugar
3 eggs
12 ounces fig preserves
    (see recipe, p. 83)
½ cup buttermilk
1 teaspoon vanilla extract
1 cup chopped pecans, optional

Preheat oven to 350°F.

Grease and flour a 10-inch fluted tube pan. In a bowl, sift together flour, spices, soda, and salt. Set aside. In a large mixing bowl, beat together oil and sugar. Add the eggs and beat until smooth and honey colored. Mix in the fig preserves. Add the dry ingredients alternately with buttermilk and beat until thoroughly moistened. Add vanilla extract. Add pecans, if desired.

Bake for 1 hour, until a toothpick inserted into the center of the cake comes out clean. Allow to cool in the pan for 10 minutes. Turn onto a serving plate and pour buttermilk glaze over hot cake. Serve warm or at room temperature.

Buttermilk Glaze

³/₄ CUP

¼ cup melted butter
1 cup sugar
½ cup buttermilk
½ teaspoon baking soda
1 tablespoon light corn syrup
1 teaspoon vanilla extract

Combine all ingredients but vanilla in heavy saucepan; bring to boil while stirring constantly. Boil 4 minutes. Remove from heat, add vanilla and pour over inverted hot cake.

thick and 5 inches in diameter. Spoon a tablespoon of the filling into the center of each round, brush edges of dough with water, and fold dough over filling to form a half-circle. Press the edges together with tines of a fork until well sealed. Trim any rough edges.

Put enough oil in a deep, heavy skillet to cover the bottom by an inch. Turn heat to medium high (the oil should be 375°F). Put several pies into the hot oil (enough to fill the pan without crowding) and fry about 3 to 4 minutes. Turn over and continue cooking for 3 to 4 more minutes, being careful not to scorch the pies. Drain briefly on paper towels and dust with confectioners' sugar. Serve warm or at room temperature.

For those with a fear of frying, you can bake these pies instead. The crust will be drier and not as flaky. Place baking rack in upper third of oven and preheat oven to 350°F. Put pies on ungreased cookie sheet, brush with melted butter, and bake until lightly browned, about 12 to 15 minutes. Dust with confectioners' sugar.

FRIED FRUIT PIES

This winter recipe will give you an idea of the consistency that the fruit filling should have, but fresh fruit works wonderfully too.

12 PIES

4 cups dried fruit (peaches, apples, apricots)
1 cup sugar
3 cups all-purpose flour
1 teaspoon salt
1 tablespoon sugar
⅔ cup shortening or lard
1 egg, lightly beaten
5 to 7 tablespoons ice water
Vegetable oil for frying

Put fruit, sugar, and enough water to cover in heavy saucepan. Simmer over low heat until fruit is tender, 45 minutes to 1 hour. Drain off cooking liquid and mash fruit. You should have 3 cups of fruit with little juice. Set aside.

In a medium bowl, sift together flour, salt, and sugar. Cut shortening into flour mixture with two knives or a pastry blender until mixture resembles coarse meal. Mix the egg and the water in a separate bowl. Make a well in the center of the dough and add the egg mixture. Stir until a soft dough forms.

Flour hands and divide dough into 12 balls. On floured surface, roll out each ball into a circle ⅛-inch

Fig Preserves

"By guess and by gosh" is the way my mother describes the method of preparing these preserves. Cooking the fig preserves for only 9 minutes seems an arbitrary number. But it must be the key because her preserves are always perfect. If, after the second cooking, the syrup seems too thin, remove the figs and reduce the syrup to a thicker consistency.

THREE 8-OUNCE JARS

½ cup water
3 cups whole figs, with stems
½ cup sugar
½ lemon, sliced thinly, ¹⁄₁₆- to ⅛-inch thick

In a medium saucepan, bring all of the ingredients to a boil. Boil for 9 minutes. Take the pan off the heat, cover, and let sit overnight. The next day, boil for 9 more minutes, uncovered, and let cool. With a slotted spoon, remove the figs from the syrup and place a third of the batch in a sterile 8-ounce jar. Cover with syrup and a slice of lemon. Seal and place in the refrigerator until ready to use.

A Much about Muchness

M y mother, Pam, and I were always warmly welcomed into Aunt Florence's parlor while everyone else was accepted under sufferance. Now I know why. She never accepted the rest of my mother's family, the Ireland clan. Differing so greatly from the world where she grew up, the Irelands were boisterous, party-loving, practical jokers. She married my Uncle Teenan before she even knew the relations and advised me against any future foolhardiness. She had met Teenan, fallen hopelessly in love, and married him after a short courtship. He moved her from her beloved Baltimore to Alamance County in rural North Carolina and built them a little house where they lived until he died. Then Aunt Florence sold the house (refusing to sell it to the Irelands, even though it adjoined their property), packed her bags, and hightailed it back to Baltimore.

Aunt Florence maintained, over the years, a silent and obsessive competition in baking with the Irelands. Her most prized and famous dessert, jelly roll, showed up once a year at Mamaw's birthday. It was meant to outdo her acquired relatives, and it always always did.

Jelly Roll

I have always thought the swirl of jelly makes the jelly roll the most beautiful cake. And it even tastes as good as it looks.

8 SERVINGS

3 eggs
½ cup sugar
½ cup all-purpose flour
½ teaspoon baking powder
¼ teaspoon salt
1 tablespoon hot water
1 cup confectioners' sugar to dredge
1 cup warm jelly or jam

Preheat oven to 425°F.

Line a 9 × 12-inch jelly roll pan with baking parchment, or use a nonstick jelly roll pan. Combine the eggs and sugar in a large bowl, set it over a pan of hot water and whisk until light and creamy. The mixture should be stiff enough to retain the impression of the whisk for a few seconds. Remove the bowl from the heat and continue to whisk until cool. Sift half the flour with baking powder and salt over the mixture and fold in very lightly, using a spatula. Add the remaining flour in the same way, and lightly stir in the hot water. Pour the mixture into the prepared pan, allowing it to run over the whole surface. Bake near the top of the oven for 7 to 9 minutes until golden brown, well risen and firm.

Pink Swirl

If you make your own jellies or jams, jelly roll is a beautiful way to use them. I make my own when I can, but I am lucky enough to have a dear friend, Pansy, in England, who twice a year will send seedless raspberry jam made by Wilkin & Sons (heavenly and a lovely dark pink color!). Try fig preserves or any one of your favorites.

Meanwhile, have ready a sheet of waxed paper liberally sprinkled with confectioners' sugar. Place the paper over a tea towel lightly wrung out in hot water. Turn the cake quickly out onto the paper, trim off the crusty edges with a sharp knife, and give them to a small child to nibble. Spread the sponge cake with warm jelly or jam. Roll up with the aid of the paper, making the first turn firmly so that the whole cake will roll out evenly and have a good shape when finished, but roll more lightly after this first turn. Dredge the cake with confectioners' sugar and cool on a cake rack. Cut into 1-inch slices, and serve with whipped cream or fresh berries.

Simple Pleasure

We were a pride of cousins. On occasions when we all had gathered from various corners of the South, my grandmother's house would echo with the cacophony of thirteen grandchildren. Once we took two of Bett's babies, still in diapers, sledding with us in the woods. We found a hill that provided the most exciting sled ride in my memory. It made children of our parents, and we all sledded together, even all the moms who usually stayed indoors with the babies. By dusk, exhilarated, wet, and cold, we trudged home. A warm fire and Burnt-Sugar Cake welcomed us back.

Burnt-Sugar Cake with Burnt-Sugar Frosting

This was Daddy's favorite birthday cake.

10 TO 12 SERVINGS

Syrup:

⅔ cup sugar
⅔ cup boiling water

Cake:

½ cup butter, softened
1½ cups sugar
1 teaspoon vanilla
2 eggs
2½ cups sifted cake flour
3 teaspoons baking powder
½ teaspoon salt
¾ cup cold water
3 tablespoons burnt-sugar syrup

Preheat oven to 375°F.

To make the syrup, in a heavy skillet, heat sugar over low heat, stirring constantly, until it melts and becomes dark brown. Slowly add boiling water. Stir until dissolved and boil to reduce to ¾ cup.

To make the cake, in a medium bowl, cream butter and sugar. Add vanilla and eggs and beat well. In a separate bowl, mix together flour, baking powder, and salt. Add dry ingredients to the egg mixture, alternately with the water, beating until smooth. Add 3 tablespoons of the burnt-sugar syrup and beat for 5 minutes at medium speed. Pour into two 9-inch greased and waxed paper–lined pans and bake for 20 minutes, or until a toothpick inserted in the center comes out clean. Cool 10 minutes in the pans, then turn onto cake racks and cool completely. Frost with Burnt-Sugar Frosting.

Burnt-Sugar Frosting

2 egg whites, at room temperature
1¼ cups brown sugar
3 to 4 tablespoons burnt sugar syrup
¼ cup cold water
Pinch of salt
1 teaspoon vanilla

Combine egg whites, brown sugar, water, sugar syrup, and salt and beat one minute to blend. Pour into the top of a double boiler and cook, beating constantly, until frosting forms stiff peaks, about 7 minutes. Don't overcook. Remove the top of the double boiler to cool the surface. Add vanilla and beat until frosting reaches spreading consistency, about 2 minutes.

CHRISTMAS ORANGE CAKE

This is a big cake and needs large mixing bowls. It can also be made into 3 or 4 loaf cakes if desired. And it gets better as it ages. It can be frozen, stored in the refrigerator (better hide it), eaten at room temperature, or slightly chilled.

12 TO 16 SERVINGS

1 pound orange slice candies, cut up
1 pound pitted dates, cut up
2 cups chopped pecans or walnuts or
    a mixture of the two
1 tablespoon grated orange rind
    (reserve orange pulp and juice for glaze)
4 cups all-purpose flour, divided
1 cup butter, softened
2 cups granulated sugar
4 eggs
1 tablespoon vanilla extract
1 teaspoon baking soda
2 teaspoons baking powder
½ teaspoon salt
½ cup buttermilk
3½ ounces grated coconut

Preheat oven to 275°F. Grease and flour a 12-inch tube pan. Place a shallow pan of hot water on the bottom rack of the oven. Combine orange slices, dates, nuts, orange rind, and 2 cups of the flour in a large bowl. In another large bowl, cream butter and sugar. Add eggs and vanilla, beating well. In a separate bowl, sift together remaining two cups of flour with soda, baking powder, and salt. Add flour mixture to butter mixture alternately with buttermilk until well blended. Add nut mixture and coconut and mix well. Pour batter into a greased pan and place on the middle rack of the oven. Bake 1 hour and 15 minutes, until a cake tester or straw comes out clean. Spoon glaze over cake while it is still hot. Chill overnight and remove from the pan.

Glaze

Juice of 3 oranges and some pulp
½ cup sugar

Combine oranges and sugar in a medium saucepan and boil until sugar is dissolved. Pour over the warm cake.

Sugar-Crust Pound Cake with Sherry Sauce

The most basic of recipes with a satisfying crusty top.

12 TO 16 SERVINGS

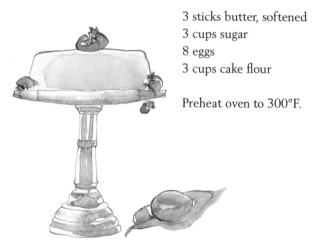

3 sticks butter, softened
3 cups sugar
8 eggs
3 cups cake flour

Preheat oven to 300°F.

In a medium bowl, cream butter and sugar. Add eggs one at a time, beating well after each addition. Add the flour in small amounts at a time, beating well after each addition. Bake in a well-greased 10- to 12-inch tube or bundt pan for 1 hour and 15 minutes. Do not open oven door until cake has been baking for an hour. Cool and turn out onto the serving plate. Serve sliced with sherry sauce spooned over.

Sherry Sauce

³⁄₄ CUP

2 eggs
1 cup sugar
2 tablespoons of butter
½ cup dry sherry
Pinch of salt

Beat eggs and sugar together in the top of a double boiler. Cook over boiling water until thick; stir in butter, sherry, and salt. Serve warm.

My Aunt Susan made her first cake all by herself when she was a mere six years old, using all the old methods her mother had taught her: measuring wet and dry ingredients accurately, sifting, creaming, breaking eggs, adding dry and wet ingredients four to three, beating well after each addition. The finished product was sort of flat because she forgot the flour, but she and her brother ate it frosted with chocolate icing and accompanied by cambric tea (a mixture of hot water, milk, and sugar, with a touch of tea) and pronounced it a success. Thus began a series of cake-baking triumphs.

Alas, she fell in love with a man who loved pies.

As I Like It

When things get tough and my eyes are like a frog's eyes in a hailstorm from crying, I go into the kitchen. Baking seems to set the world right side up again. Out of my despair I have prepared the most beautiful desserts, like my Warm Chocolate Cake—tender, deeply chocolate, and redemptive. The kitchen can be a place of comfort and control like no other for me. Tools and materials are neatly stored and organized, and the skills I've privately honed and used here always produce a calm in the midst of almost any calamity. Sometimes I mimic my grandmother's assuredness in dancing about the space and try on all of her stylistic dashes, pantomime my father's way of setting up ingredients, conjure up my mother's rules of timing and attentiveness. But it is clearly my space. Let no one enter when I need the comforts of such order. Maybe this explains why the kitchen can be the site of worship—and crimes of passion.

WARM CHOCOLATE CAKE

I prefer this cake cooked all the way through so it isn't gooey in the middle, even though that's the trend these days. But if it does come out gooey, so what, it still is a pleasure and a comfort.

4 SERVINGS

½ cup butter
4 ounces bittersweet chocolate
2 eggs
2 egg yolks
½ cup sugar
2 teaspoons all-purpose flour
Confectioners' sugar for dusting cake

Preheat oven to 450°F.

Put butter and chocolate in the top of a double boiler and heat over simmering water until chocolate has almost melted. Set aside. In a medium bowl, mix eggs, yolks, and sugar until very light and thick, and will make ribbons when dropped from a spoon, or when it's twice its volume. Add chocolate mixture and combine well. Beat in flour until just combined. Pour batter into 4 buttered and floured baking dishes (like custard cups) or an 8 × 8-inch glass baking dish. Place dishes on baking sheet and bake for 8 to 10 minutes or until the outer rim has set but the middle is still soft. For a firmer center, bake 2 to 4 minutes longer. Invert each dish on a plate and let cool for 15 seconds. Lift up one corner of the dish and the cake will fall onto the plate. Dust with confectioners' sugar, and serve with Raspberry Sauce (p. 116).

Pam's Persimmon-Apple Cake

8 TO 12 SERVINGS

½ cup butter
1½ cups sugar
2 eggs
1 teaspoon vanilla
1½ cups peeled, grated apple
1 cup persimmon pulp (see p. 32)
1½ teaspoons fresh lemon juice
1 teaspoon baking soda
2 cups all-purpose flour
1 teaspoon salt
1 teaspoon cinnamon
¼ teaspoon nutmeg
¼ teaspoon cloves
¼ teaspoon ginger
2 teaspoons grated orange zest

A staple in the early fall after the first frost. Heavenly when hot from the oven.

Preheat oven to 350°F.

In a mixing bowl, cream butter with sugar. Add eggs, vanilla, and apple. In a separate bowl, combine persimmon pulp, lemon juice, and baking soda. Add to the creamed mixture. In a third bowl, mix together flour, salt, spices, and orange zest. Blend into the persimmon mixture. Pour into a greased and floured bundt pan and bake for 1 hour. Cool 10 minutes, invert onto a plate and dust with confectioners' sugar.

Serve unadorned or with Bourbon Sauce (p. 116).

Moving

Lured by a better job, in spite of the miserable upheaval it caused my mother, my father moved us from Statesville back to Charlotte for the second time in as many years. He rented a modest house for us in a new suburb. Charlotte was still  a naive, sleepy town like so many other Southern towns before the unrest of the '60s. My sister and I roamed the neighborhood with the other kids. On Sundays, my father, exhausted from his new job, immersed himself in television and the papers on his only day off. My mother was left to her own devices.

That winter was particularly cold with endless gray, still days. Accustomed to the constant activity of farm life with relatives and animals, barns and warm fires, my mother often felt lonely and estranged in this new life. There was nothing quite like the melancholy of a Southern suburb on a Sunday afternoon in the winter. Mother's way of warding off gloom was to take on something a bit challenging in the kitchen. It calmed her to create something as surprising as cream puffs. They steamed up the windows, made the house smell like vanilla beans, and enveloped us in a sense of well-being and cheer.

CREAM PUFFS

Like a profiterole, only American and Southern.

12 LARGE PUFFS

1 cup water
½ cup shortening
⅛ teaspoon salt
1 cup all-purpose flour, sifted
3 eggs, beaten

Dessert is a happy ending.

If you choose to succumb to the guilty pleasure of it all and feel defeated, take a walk around the block and get a little perspective.

Preheat oven to 450°F.

In a medium saucepan bring water to a boil. Add shortening and salt and stir over medium heat until mixture boils. Turn heat to low and add flour all at once and stir vigorously with a wooden spoon until the mixture leaves the sides of the pan, 30 seconds to 1 minute. Do not overstir. Remove from the heat and add eggs one at a time, beating thoroughly after each addition. Drop by large spoonfuls (1 tablespoon is too small) on an ungreased cookie sheet. Bake at 450°F for 20 minutes, then reduce the heat to 350°F and bake 20 minutes longer. Remove from the oven and place puffs on a rack to cool. When cool, cut off the tops with a sharp knife. At the moment of serving, fill the bottoms with custard and replace the tops. Spoon Hot Fudge Sauce (p. 117) over each puff.

Vanilla Custard

3 CUPS

6 egg yolks
⅔ cup sugar
2 tablespoons flour, sifted
2 cups milk
1 vanilla bean

Using an electric mixer on high speed, beat egg yolks with the sugar in a medium bowl until the mixture is very thick, pale yellow, and forms a ribbon when the beater is lifted. Whisk in the flour.

In a 2-quart stainless steel saucepan, scald the milk with the vanilla bean. Pour about ¼ of the hot milk into the egg yolk mixture, whisking continuously. Return this mixture to the saucepan, combining with remaining milk. Cook over medium heat for 5 minutes, whisking constantly, until the mixture thickens and bubbles in the middle. Let it bubble for only a few seconds, but do not boil. Strain into a bowl and cover immediately with plastic wrap pressed down on the top to prevent a skin from forming. Chill for 30 minutes. Will keep refrigerated for 1 week.

Chilled &
Spirited
Desserts

Spring Forward

My visits to my grandmother's farm during summer vacation were capped with a picnic at the spring. Back in the '40s a barbeque had been built there, and later someone added a picnic table. We all walked there from the house—even my grandmother with her bad knees. We cousins, dizzy, danced ahead through the leafy woods. The spring was down a large hill covered with hickory and redbud and moss-covered boulders. It was the unpolluted source that fed two ponds, one small and one large. There was an old metal dipper hanging on a nail by the tree and we drank the cool water that conveniently pooled in one spot.

We spread out a supper of hot dogs, chili, and coleslaw, then walked a little way to the small pond, skipped stones, threw in a line from our crude fishing poles, and waited for the hot dogs to be roasted. We competed to find the most perfect roasting stick for marshmallows, and then devoured our hot dogs. I couldn't wait for the end of the meal. Finally, Mamaw sliced slivers of Sugar-Crust Pound Cake, which everybody ate with their hands, and then pulled out a bag of marshmallows. A minute next to the flame was all you needed to turn your marshmallow into molten sweetness.

But we always saved room for the best part of the meal. We took turns cranking the freezer for Aunt Bett's peach ice cream. It tested the strength of every cousin's young arms and led to another competition of stamina. Everyone was awarded a prize: a big bowl of fragrant, sweet ice cream.

PEACH ICE CREAM

I promise the pudding will simplify your life because that is what Aunt Bett had to do. She had so many children, nieces, and nephews, and the demand for this ice cream was so great, that she had to work out a foolproof shortcut.

1 GALLON OR 18 SERVINGS

8 to 10 ripe peaches
1 cup sugar
½ package instant vanilla pudding
1 can sweetened condensed milk
1 pint heavy cream
1½ quarts whole milk
6 eggs

Dip each peach in boiling water to remove skins. Slice the peaches and toss with the sugar in a medium bowl. Set aside.

Mix together the pudding, the condensed milk, cream, and whole milk in a heavy-bottomed saucepan. Beat the eggs in a separate bowl and add to the milk mixture. Cook slowly until the mixture barely coats the back of a wooden spoon. Remove from the stove and stir in the peaches. Freeze in ice-cream maker according to manufacturer's instructions.

SNOW CREAM

Should follow making snow angels.

10 SERVINGS

¾ can sweetened condensed milk
½ cup sugar
2 cups milk
6 to 8 cups clean snow

Beat together all ingredients and add snow until it's the consistency of ice cream. Taste as you go along for desired sweetness.

FROZEN FRUIT COMPOTE

A mélange a trois. To be eaten with someone you love.

4 TO 6 SERVINGS

1 cup crushed pineapple
1 small can pineapple juice
1 tablespoon butter
1 tablespoon all-purpose flour
2 tablespoons lemon juice
1 tablespoon sugar
Dash of salt
1 egg, beaten
½ cup miniature marshmallows
1 cup sour cream
½ cup pecans, broken
1 cup fresh strawberries, sliced
1 cup bananas, sliced

Drain pineapple, reserving ¾ cup juice. (There never seems to be enough juice in canned pineapple so I buy additional pineapple juice.) In a 1-quart saucepan, melt butter, and stir in the flour. Remove from heat and gradually stir in the pineapple juice. Cook over medium heat, stirring constantly until thickened. Cook 2 more minutes. Add lemon juice, sugar, and salt. Blend a small amount of hot mixture into egg, then pour back into hot mixture. Return to heat. Cook 1 minute, but do not boil. Remove from heat and stir in marshmallows until they are melted. Cool for 30 minutes. Fold in sour cream. Add pineapple, nuts, strawberries, and bananas and stir until blended. Pour into a 9 × 12-inch pan, cover and freeze for two hours. Remove from the freezer a few minutes before serving and slice into squares.

AMBROSIA

Upon saying fare-thee-well to the fruits of summer, think of the food of the gods.

4 SERVINGS

3 oranges
½ cup Grand Marnier
2 plums, pitted and cut into ¼-inch wedges
4 stawberries, topped and diced
½ cup shredded coconut

Cut the top and bottom off the oranges. Score the oranges in quarters and pry off the peel. Scrape all the pith from the rind and cut into thin julienne slices to make approximately ¼ cup. Section the oranges carefully, retaining any juice while peeling the membrane off the sections. Marinate the oranges and the julienne in the Grand Marnier and their juice in the refrigerator for 4 hours, turning with a fork from time to time.

In a small bowl, mix the plums, strawberries, and coconut. Remove the orange sections from the Grand Marnier, divide evenly into 4 servings, and fan them out onto a dessert plate. Remove the slivers of orange peel and put aside. In the center of the fan, place a scoop of the plum, strawberries, and coconut mixture. Pour a little of the Grand Marnier and juice mixture over the ambrosia. Garnish with a cluster of the marinated orange peel.

Note: The orange and coconut combination is the anchor to this dessert, but you can vary its composition with grapes, mango, kiwi, or whatever looks fresh at the market.

There are three kinds of dessert people. Fruit, chocolate, and custard. I know several of each kind. Most dessert people are passionate about their kind. Even Puritans who were passionate about *no* pleasure delighted in sugar, molasses, and rum.

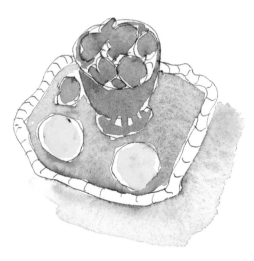

Communion

*R*arely were we children encouraged to join the domain of grown-up company. Most of the time when we visited Ms. Ayres and my grandmother, we were taken into the kitchen where the servants prepared the meals, the place in the large house where they were most comfortable talking and laughing. On the other side of the swinging door, the house immediately was formal, quiet, velveted, rich. The kitchen was a string of three rooms along the back of the house that connected to the servants' stairwell. It was always in order—clean and gleaming white with linoleum floors and shiny porcelain.

"Would you like to go out to the kitchen with Annie and have some cream?" my grandmother would ask when she needed to discuss something important with my father. My sister and I would be led through the opulent front rooms to the back of the house, where Annie, the cook, served us bowls of ice cream at the white enamel table.

By the time I was twelve, we were allowed once a year to have dessert with the grown-ups in order to experience my grandmother's wine jelly. It was the only thing my grandmother cooked. She served it ceremoniously at New Year's along with the details of the painstaking process of preparing it, down to how long it took the chauffeur to drive to the store to get the sherry. Alcohol was never ever served in our Baptist-to-the-bone family, so the allowance of it in the dessert was something indeed.

WINE JELLY

Wine jelly is the most grown-up dessert that I know of.
I didn't like it as a child, but knew better than to say so.
I love it as a grown-up. My grandmother always served
it with her custard sauce.

8 TO 10 SERVINGS

5 envelopes of unflavored gelatin
2 cups cold water
4 cups boiling water
4½ cups sugar
2 cups white wine
1 lemon, juiced and strained
2 oranges, juiced and strained

Soften gelatin in cold water for 5 minutes. Bring hot water and sugar to boil. Remove from heat, add gelatin and blend well. Cool. Stir in wine, lemon juice, and orange juice. Pour into a mold or individual glasses. Refrigerate until firm, about four to six hours. Spoon wine jelly into goblets, cover with the custard, and top with whipped cream.

Custard Sauce

6 egg yolks, at room temperature
    and lightly beaten
⅔ cup sugar
Pinch of salt
2 cups half-and-half, at room temperature
2 tablespoons sherry or brandy, or
    1 teaspoon vanilla

In the bottom of a double boiler, bring one inch of water (water must not touch top pan) to simmer over medium heat. In the top of a double boiler, beat together egg yolks, sugar, and salt until thick and light-colored. Gradually add half-and-half. Heat, stirring constantly, until mixture is somewhat thickened and coats a spoon. (Mixture must not come to a boil or it will curdle.) Remove from heat; add sherry or brandy or vanilla. Chill.

Poached Peaches with Whole Peppercorns

Daddy peppers everything: conversations, fruits, main courses. He added whole peppercorns to these peaches to add a pleasant spiciness to their syrup.

4 SERVINGS

4 small whole peaches
1½ cups sugar
1 teaspoon whole peppercorns
2 cups water
One 2-inch piece of vanilla bean,
    split lengthwise
Juice of 1 lemon
2 tablespoons sherry, optional

Dip peaches in boiling water and remove peels. Cut in half, remove pit, and place peaches cut side down in a saucepan just large enough to hold them comfortably. Sprinkle with sugar and peppercorns. Add vanilla bean and pour water and lemon juice over peaches.

Cover the pan and slowly bring almost to a boil over medium heat. Lower temperature immediately, and simmer very gently for 15 to 20 minutes until the fruit is tender and cooked through. After 10 minutes, gently turn the peaches over with a wooden spoon and continue simmering for 5 to 10 minutes. Add sherry, if desired, and stir. Place 2 peach halves on each plate and ladle sauce over the fruit. Garnish with whipped cream.

Figs in Spiced Wine

A delicious, simple ending to a summer meal.

4 SERVINGS

¼ cup dry sauterne
2 tablespoons sugar
1 tablespoon lemon juice
Dash cinnamon
Dash crushed cloves
12 medium, whole figs, stems on

In a small saucepan, heat together sauterne, sugar, and lemon juice. Cook, stirring until the sugar dissolves. Do not boil. Stir in spices. Put the figs in a deep bowl and pour wine mixture over them. Macerate in the refrigerator for 4 hours. Divide fruit between bowls, pouring the wine mixture over them. Garnish with a sprig of thyme or mint.

Note: Three medium peaches, peeled and sliced, can be used in place of figs.

Humble Pie

I had authentic fried pies only twice as a child, and I will never forget either time. Both were in remote country places where one suspects moonshine was still being produced. The first was at an auction way out in the country, a good hour's drive from Statesville. The very air seemed so unfamiliar and so rural that Mother and I felt like cosmopolitan city folk. The lady selling fried pies was a country wife, pink cheeked and silver haired. The apple pies, wrapped in waxed paper and placed carefully on her oilcloth-covered table, were twenty-five cents apiece. I tasted one, and it was the essence of tart-but-sweet apple, the crust flavorful and crisp. I bought another. My mother bought an ironstone cake pedestal.

The next time I had a fried pie was at Uncle William's mother's house in Gibsonville. I watched as Winnie rolled out the pies, loaded them up with her canned peaches, folded them over into triangles,

crimped the edges with a fork, and gently slid them into hot oil.
When they were nicely golden, she lifted them out onto paper towels
and sprinkled them liberally with confectioners' sugar. Unable to
resist and barely able to wait till they cooled, I ate two.

Fried pies may not be appropriately soigné at modern dinner
parties unless you call them tartes frites or, perhaps, dessert
samosas. I've filled them with just-picked strawberries macerated
in sugar and balsamic vinegar, fresh pears poached in sauterne,
and peaches sautéed in a little butter and sugar. They are still best
on picnics. And to give them more authenticity, I wrap them in
separate pieces of waxed paper—like little country presents.

Coconut Custard Pie

As a ten-year-old baker, I began making this pie for my father, who declared it his absolute favorite.

Two 8-inch pies, or 12 servings

¼ cup butter, melted
1½ cups sugar
3 eggs, beaten
1 tablespoon all-purpose flour
1½ cups milk
1 cup grated coconut
2 teaspoons vanilla
Two 8-inch unbaked pie shells

Preheat oven to 350°F.

Pour butter over sugar in a medium bowl and mix well. Add eggs, flour, milk, coconut, and vanilla and mix well. Divide mixture between the 2 unbaked pie shells. Bake in oven until nut-brown and custard has set up and is cracked around the edges, about 40 to 45 minutes. Serve unadorned with a good cup of coffee.

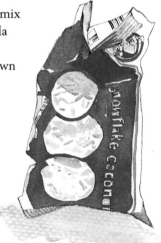

Note: These days I like to use unsweetened coconut from a health food store or frozen coconut, but canned coconut is what we traditionally used.

Strike

The second piece of pumpkin pie caused all the trouble. After lunch under the lone shade tree, James, my mother's elder brother, got up and ambled back over to the plow to continue cutting the corn. They still had another field to finish, and he knew that in spite of the hot October day, Mamaw was expecting them to finish it all. L.A., the youngest, had finished off his first piece of pie and was contemplating a second. He kept his eyes on the front porch just in case Mamaw should appear to ask what in the blazes was taking them so long to plow under the shocks of corn. He had the pie up to his mouth when he saw the front porch door swing open and Mamaw's stout figure appear. L.A. jumped up to dart back to the field, and as he did, the copperhead struck him right in the leg.

James got to him first. It was a fierce bite; the swelling had already started by the time Mamaw reached him. The car was not running, and the only way to get him to Dr. Kernodle was for

James to unhitch Beck the mule from the plow and lead him with L.A. slouched on top to the doctor's office.

The trip was long and slow. The poison and heat caused L.A. to pass out. He was very sick for several days, but he survived. While he recovered, he was allowed to rest in bed and eat as much pie as he liked.

Pumpkin Chiffon Pie

Lighter and more wondrous than the traditional pumpkin pie.

8 SERVINGS

1 tablespoon (1 envelope) unflavored gelatin
¼ cup cold water
3 egg yolks, slightly beaten
2 cups sugar, divided
1 cup pumpkin puree
1½ cups milk
¼ teaspoon salt
¼ teaspoon cloves
¼ teaspoon ginger
¼ teaspoon cinnamon
¼ teaspoon nutmeg
3 egg whites
1 graham cracker crust (recipe follows)

In a small bowl, soften gelatin in water for 5 minutes. In a medium bowl, mix together egg yolks, 1 cup of the sugar, pumpkin, milk, salt, and spices. Add the gelatin. Cook over low heat, or in a double boiler, stirring constantly until mixture thickens. Take off heat and set aside to cool. In a separate bowl, beat egg whites until stiff and slowly incorporate the remaining sugar. Fold egg whites into cooled pumpkin mixture, mixing lightly. Pour into graham cracker crust and serve warm or chilled with whipped cream.

Graham Cracker Crust

MAKES ONE 9-INCH SHELL

1½ cups fine graham cracker crumbs
¼ cup sugar
½ cup butter, melted

In a medium bowl, mix crumbs and sugar together. Add the butter and stir with a fork to distribute evenly. Line a pie pan with the mixture by pressing it firmly into place with the back of a tablespoon. Chill for 20 minutes to set, or bake at 350°F for 10 minutes. Cool before adding filling.

SHOOFLY PIE

The American Dictionary of Slang gives the definition of shoofly as "a mild expression of surprise." This pie is the definition of pleasant surprise.

8 SERVINGS

Filling:

½ tablespoon baking
 soda
¾ cup boiling water
½ cup molasses
1 egg yolk, beaten well

One 9-inch unbaked
 pie shell

Topping:

¾ cup all-purpose flour
½ teaspoon
 cinnamon
⅛ teaspoon nutmeg
⅛ teaspoon ginger
⅛ teaspoon cloves
½ cup brown sugar
½ teaspoon salt
2 tablespoons
 chilled butter

Preheat oven to 400° F.

In a medium bowl, dissolve the baking soda in the hot water. Add the molasses and egg yolk and mix well.

Combine all the dry topping ingredients in a medium bowl. Work in the butter with two knives or a pastry blender until the mixture becomes crumbly.

Pour the filling into the unbaked pie shell. Sprinkle with the crumb topping. Bake at 400°F for about 10 minutes, or until the crust is lightly browned. Reduce heat to 325°F and bake until firm, another 10 to 15 minutes. Serve with an herbal sprig or whipped cream.

Lemon Meringue Pie

Lemon meringue pie, like banana pudding, is one of those sublimely Southern sweets that men love and more often declare as their favorite dessert.

8 SERVINGS

Meringue:

6 egg whites at room
   temperature
¾ teaspoon cream
   of tartar
¾ cup sugar
⅛ teaspoon salt
1 teaspoon vanilla

Filling:

½ cup cornstarch
3 tablespoons all-
   purpose flour
1½ cups sugar
1¼ cups water
2 eggs
6 egg yolks (reserve egg
   whites for meringue)
¼ teaspoon salt
3 tablespoons butter
½ cup fresh lemon juice
Grated zest of two
   lemons
½ teaspoon vanilla

One 9-inch blind-
   baked pie shell

Preheat oven to 325°F.

For the meringue, beat egg whites and cream of tartar until foamy in a large mixing bowl. Gradually add ¾ cup sugar and beat until stiff but not dry (still glossy). Stir in ⅛ teaspoon salt and 1 teaspoon vanilla. Set aside while assembling the filling.

For the filling, stir together cornstarch, flour, and sugar in a medium saucepan. Stir in the water and cook over medium heat until thick, stirring constantly. Remove from heat. Mix eggs and yolks together in small bowl. Stir ½ cup of the hot mixture into egg mixture, and then stir egg mixture into remaining hot filling. Return to a boil and cook three to four minutes, stirring constantly.

Remove from heat and stir in salt, butter, lemon juice, zest, and vanilla. Pour into pie shell. Spread meringue on *hot* lemon filling, being sure to cover (seal in) all of the filling. Make peaks and swirls using the back of a spoon. Bake in the lower third of the oven for 30 minutes or until lightly browned. Put it in a windowsill to cool. Serve at room temperature.

Note: The meringue must be spread over hot lemon mixture, so move quickly and have your shell blind-baked and your filling and meringue ingredients organized before you start.

Shine On

I n Carolina, I have seen a full moon rise crimson in
a late December sky. In the spring, a big ol' ochre orb
could move one to tears. Our summer nights at the beach
were punctuated by at least one opaque white moon as big as
the sky that lit our paths next to the dark, thundering Atlantic.

By the time October rolled around and we thought we'd seen it all,
out glided the biggest, palest butternut queen of the night, and
we'd realize we were just silly old humans compared to the wonders
of a Southern night sky. Guess that's why there's a moon pie.

Moon Pie

The commercial kind—sickly marshmallows sandwiched between undistinguished chocolate wafers—does not a moon pie make. This moon pie is a dreamy mocha cream.

8 SERVINGS

2 cups milk
¼ cup instant coffee granules
¾ cup sugar
⅓ cup all-purpose flour
¼ teaspoon salt
1 ounce unsweetened chocolate
2 eggs
1 egg yolk
1 tablespoon butter, melted
1 teaspoon vanilla
One 9-inch blind-baked pie shell

Herbal Sprigs

thyme

mint

rosemary

In a medium saucepan scald milk, warming it to just below boiling. Remove from heat and add the coffee. Strain. In a medium bowl, sift sugar, flour, and salt together and stir into milk. Cook in a double boiler over boiling water until thickened, stirring constantly. Add chocolate and continue cooking 10 minutes, or until the chocolate is melted, stirring occasionally. Remove the mixture from the double boiler. In a small bowl, beat eggs and egg yolk slightly. Add ¼ of the hot milk mixture to the beaten eggs, then add the egg mixture to the remaining milk and return to the double boiler. Cook, stirring constantly, for 2 minutes. Remove from heat and add butter and vanilla. Let cool for 20 minutes. Pour into pie shell and chill. Serve with a dollop of whipped cream and an herbal sprig.

Puddings

&

Custards

Papaw

My grandfather Ireland was a curious fellow. I have never gotten a straight answer about his occupation. I do know that he was a darn good fisherman and an ever ready huntsman. As a young man he single-handedly wrestled the Ireland property back from the chokehold of the tax collectors, his most heroic deed. As a deputy sheriff, nothing terrible happened on his watch, but no impressive stories were ever recounted about him saving someone or the community from harm.

Over the years I've pieced together that he was an idle farmer, full of wisdom and county lore, who mostly sat in his chair, chewed tobacco, and took long walks with his dog around the remaining hundred or so Ireland acres. (No one knows exactly how the Irelands came into the farm either. Some say that my great-grandfather won three hundred acres in a poker game.)

But the strangely sweet story of Papaw's death is true, because I was there. He went out one September Saturday for his ritual constitutional and never returned. He probably lay down alongside one of his fields under a turning cherry tree to take a nap and just didn't wake up.

My grandmother and I had just baked a cherry pudding from the fruit of that very grove and only began to worry when Papaw didn't return for lunch. In the afternoon we saw his dog loping sideways to the house.

He led my anxious Mamaw and me back to the field where Papaw lay peacefully among the tender rural colors.

MOM'S CHERRY PUDDING

My mother and her oeuvre were not directly influenced by French cuisine in the '50s and '60s, so this pudding unknowingly resembles the now popular French clafouti.

6 SERVINGS

2 tablespoons butter, divided
2 cups dark cherries, washed and pitted
½ cup sugar, divided
1½ cups whole milk or half-and-half
2 eggs, beaten
6 tablespoons all-purpose flour
1 tablespoon vanilla
¼ teaspoon salt

Preheat oven to 400°F.

Butter a 9-inch glass pie pan using 1 tablespoon of the butter. Mix ¼ cup sugar with the cherries and spread over the bottom of the buttered pan. In a medium bowl make a smooth batter of the milk, eggs, 1 tablespoon melted butter, flour, salt, and vanilla. Pour the batter over the cherries. Cook for 30 minutes, reducing heat to 325°F if the top appears to be browning too fast, until filling is just set. Sprinkle copiously with confectioners' sugar. Serve warm with heavy cream.

WILD PERSIMMON PUDDING

Wash fruits gently before mashing. Use a sieve and pestle to remove skin and seeds from persimmons. You need a little more than 2 cups of whole fruits to produce 1 cup of pulp. Why go to the trouble? Because this is the most wonderful pudding I know of.

10 SERVINGS

3 cups wild persimmon pulp
2 cups milk
3 cups all-purpose flour
1 teaspoon salt
½ teaspoon (scant) cloves
½ teaspoon nutmeg
1 teaspoon cinnamon
1½ teaspoon baking powder
2 eggs
1 cup sugar
1 teaspoon vanilla
1 teaspoon lemon juice
¼ cup butter, melted
½ teaspoon baking soda in
    1 teaspoon hot water

Preheat oven to 350°F.

Stir milk into persimmon pulp. In a separate bowl, sift flour; then measure and resift with salt, spices, and baking powder. In a large bowl, beat egg until light yellow. Gradually add sugar and continue beating until creamy. Stir in vanilla and lemon juice and beat in the butter. Add the persimmon mixture alternately with the flour. Incorporate the soda and hot water mixture quickly into the pudding and blend. Pour into an $8 \times 12 \times 2$-inch buttered glass baking dish and bake for 45 to 50 minutes. Cut into squares and serve warm with whipped cream.

Diospyros virginiana

Our Persimmon desserts are traditionally made with *Diospyros virginiana*—small, wild persimmons gathered from the countryside. My sister Pam has had great success with the larger Japanese persimmons from a tree in her yard in northern California. If you are gathering the persimmons yourself, make sure you wait until after the first frost to gather the fruits that have fallen to the ground to insure that they're ripe. (Freezing ripens the fruit. If you can't wait for a frost, freeze the fruit overnight before using.)

An unripe persimmon, or one plucked from the tree, no matter how beautiful, will have the bitterest of tastes and is the meaning of pucker.

Banana Pudding

My brother-in-law prefers this dessert on his birthday instead of cake.

8 SERVINGS

Pudding:

½ cup sugar
2 tablespoons all-purpose
    flour
Dash of salt
2 cups milk
4 egg yolks
1 teaspoon vanilla
35 to 45 vanilla wafers
5 to 6 bananas, sliced
    in rounds

Meringue:

4 egg whites at room
    temperature
¾ teaspoon cream
    of tartar
¼ cup sugar
⅛ teaspoon salt
1 teaspoon vanilla

Preheat oven to 425°F.

To make pudding, combine sugar, flour, and salt in a double boiler; stir in milk. Cook, stirring constantly until thickened, about 20 minutes. Beat egg yolks in a small bowl and stir into the custard. Cook 5 minutes more. Remove from heat and stir in vanilla. Spread a small amount of custard on the bottom of a 1½-quart casserole; cover with a layer of sliced bananas. Pour about a third of the custard over the bananas. Continue to layer wafers, bananas, and custard to make 3 layers of each, ending with the custard.

To make meringue, in a large bowl beat egg whites and cream of tartar until foamy. Gradually add sugar and beat until stiff but not dry (still glossy). Stir in salt and vanilla.

Spread meringue evenly over the pudding. Make peaks and swirls with back of spoon. Bake for 5 minutes or until meringue is slightly brown. Cool slightly before serving.

Special Sugar

Vanilla sugar, made from either granulated or confectioners' sugar, makes baked desserts all the more special. Buy good quality (glossy, flexible, and highly aromatic) vanilla beans, split or whole, and bury two in a pound container of confectioners' or granulated sugar. Tightly cover the container. The sugar will be flavored and scented in a week. More sugar can be added to the container as it is used. The beans should last several months.

Raspberry Summer Pudding

The real reason we went berrying. You can substitute whatever summer berries or fruits you have on hand.

4 TO 6 SERVINGS

Filling:
2 pints raspberries
3 tablespoons sugar

Topping:
4 eggs, separated
2 teaspoons lemon zest
½ cup fresh lemon juice
3 tablespoons all-purpose flour
¼ teaspoon salt
1 cup plus 1 tablespoon sugar
2 tablespoons melted butter
1 cup milk
1 tablespoon tapioca

Place the raspberries in an 8 × 12-inch baking dish and gently toss with 3 tablespoons of the sugar. Let stand 8 hours or overnight.

Preheat oven to 350°F.

In a medium saucepan, cook the fruit over low heat for 2 to 3 minutes and let cool.

In a large bowl, whisk together the egg yolks, lemon zest, and lemon juice. Add the flour, salt, and remaining sugar and whisk until smooth. Whisk in the butter and the milk. In another bowl, beat the egg whites until stiff but not dry. Using a whisk, fold the whites into the batter.

Toss the tapioca with the raspberries. Pour the batter over the berries and bake until the pudding is lightly browned and cooked through, about 45 minutes. Serve warm or at room temperature, dusted with confectioners' sugar.

November Pudding

When winter set in and the only memory of summer in the larder was jars of preserved fruits, this was the pudding served. Simple and steamed, it is rustic elegance defined.

4 TO 6 SERVINGS

2 cups sifted all-purpose flour
1 teaspoon baking soda
1 cup plus 1 teaspoon butter, softened
1 cup light brown sugar, firmly packed
4 eggs, lightly beaten
4 heaping tablespoons raspberry jam

Sift flour and baking soda together in a medium bowl. Set aside. Cream 1 cup butter with an electric mixer until fluffy. Gradually stir in sugar, eggs, and raspberry jam until well mixed. The batter will look curdled. Sift the flour mixture over the creamed mixture, a small amount at a time, and fold in thoroughly.

Since most of us no longer plow fields or tend the livestock, our caloric needs are considerably less than they used to be. Dessert has become more indulgent. Therefore, some restraint may be necessary for waist's sake, but ruling it out of our lives altogether doesn't work either.

Lightly butter a 2-quart ceramic mold or a soufflé dish with remaining butter. Pour batter into prepared mold. Cover the mold with a tight fitting lid or seal tightly with heavy-duty aluminum foil. Place the mold in a larger pot and add enough boiling water to reach two-thirds of the way up the mold. Cover pot tightly and steam over low flame for 2 hours. Add more boiling water when necessary.

To serve, remove mold from water carefully—it will be hot—and let rest for 5 minutes. Unmold hot pudding on a serving plate and serve with Raspberry Sauce (p. 116) or Bourbon Sauce (p. 116).

APRICOT BREAD PUDDING

Heart- and belly-warming.

6 TO 8 SERVINGS

½ cup sugar
1 lemon peel, grated
2½ cups soft white bread (about 7 slices),
    crusts removed, in chunky pieces
2 cups milk
4 tablespoons butter, melted
¾ cup dried apricots, chopped
3 eggs, separated
2 whole eggs
1 teaspoon baking powder
½ teaspoon vanilla extract

Preheat oven to 350°F.

Butter a 1½-quart casserole dish. In a medium mixing bowl, mix the sugar and the lemon peel. Add the bread pieces, milk, butter, and apricots, blending well. Add the egg yolks, whole eggs, and baking powder and mix well. Beat the egg whites until they hold a stiff peak, then fold them into the mixture. Pour into the baking dish.

Place the baking dish in a pan of hot water, and bake pudding until a knife inserted in the center comes out clean, about 40 minutes. Let rest for 5 minutes, and serve with Bourbon Sauce (p. 116).

Depression Glass

There was a grand house way out in Mecklenburg County we all desperately wanted to live in. We called it the White House because Mrs. White owned it. It was a federal center hall built in the 1920s, and it sat proudly, untouchably, on a small knoll. For about a year it was empty, and while it was on the market we would wind our way to it on numerous Sunday afternoons like pilgrims. The lawn and orchards were somewhat disheveled from lack of care, but I imagined seeing the flowers in bloom from the second-story window of the room that would be mine. We all yearned to live there, but it was beyond our dreams. After a bittersweet tour of the grounds, we would pile back into the Ford, head home to our small suburban house, and bury our sorrows in chocolate pudding. Mother served it in glass goblets, the way it would have been served in the White House.

Chocolate Pudding

Much beloved and a surefire comfort food.

8 SERVINGS

2 cups sugar
1 cup cocoa
1 teaspoon salt
⅓ cup all-purpose flour
4 cups milk
4 egg yolks, slightly beaten
½ cup butter

In a heavy-bottomed pot, mix together sugar, cocoa, salt, and flour. Add cold milk and egg yolks and stir well. Cook slowly, stirring constantly until thick. Add butter and stir until blended. Pour into individual serving dishes and chill for 2 hours. Top with a cloud of whipped cream.

Kay Bennett's Deep-Dish Sweet Potato Pudding

Not just a dessert, this pudding can share center stage at Thanksgiving dinner.

8 TO 10 SERVINGS

4 pounds sweet potatoes
½ cup butter, softened
1 cup sugar
4 eggs
3 tablespoons self-rising flour
1 cup milk
¼ teaspoon salt
1 teaspoon vanilla extract
1 teaspoon coconut extract
1 cup chopped pecans
4 tablespoons dark brown sugar, packed
½ teaspoon cinnamon
Shredded coconut, optional

Preheat oven to 350°F.

In a large pan, combine potatoes with enough cold water to cover; bring them to a boil and continue cooking 30 to 40 minutes, or until tender. Drain, peel, and place potatoes in a large bowl, and with an electric mixer, beat until smooth. Add butter, sugar, eggs (one at a time), flour, milk, salt, and extracts, and beat until mixture is well combined. Divide into two 1½-quart lightly buttered soufflé dishes. In a small bowl, combine pecans, brown sugar, cinnamon, and coconut and sprinkle on top of the soufflés. Bake in middle of the oven for 1 hour.

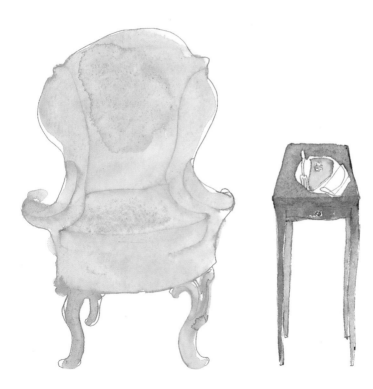

Pears in Nightshirts

Not an authentic Southern recipe at all, but a lovely dessert with a charming name that I adopted while briefly transplanted in London.

6 SERVINGS

6 pears, peeled and cored,
    with ½ inch of the bottom sliced off
    (Bartlett or Anjou, sweet but not too soft)
1½ cups apple juice
½ cup confectioners' sugar
1 tablespoon butter
1½ pounds cooking apples, peeled,
    cored, and sliced
Zest of one lemon
1 tablespoon lemon juice
3 cloves
½ cup sugar

Topping:

6 egg whites at room temperature
1 teaspoon cream of tartar
Pinch of salt
1½ cups sugar

Preheat oven to 400°F.

In a large saucepan, cook pears over low heat in apple juice for 30 minutes or until translucent. Remove from poaching liquid and sprinkle heavily with confectioners' sugar.

In heavy saucepan, melt butter and add apples, lemon zest, lemon juice, and cloves. Cook over low heat for 15 minutes until apples are very soft and most of the liquid has evaporated. Remove cloves; mash apples, add sugar to taste, starting with ¼ cup. Pour apples into a buttered 1½-quart soufflé; place pears on top.

Beat egg whites with cream of tartar and salt until thick and glossy; add sugar and beat until sugar dissolves. Pour over pears. Bake for 10 to 15 minutes.

Candy

Uncle Buddy's Wagon

*I*f you want to earn extra money for Christmas, try this. Early in December make the following: Peanut Brittle, Divinity, Pralines, and Chocolate-Covered Peanut Butter Balls.

Take one of each and place them carefully in a little white bag. Tie the bag with a red or green or gold ribbon. Put a tag on it that says "Merry Christmas from the kitchen of (your name)." Fill up a basket with the beribboned bags. Get your brother to put them in his wagon and sell them for you for five cents a bag around the neighborhood. Ask your neighbors. Visit the grocer, the hardware store, the barber shop. Do this every day after school for about three weeks, and you should accumulate a sizable amount of money, enough to buy your momma and daddy a Christmas present.

Or at least it worked for my Aunt Brenda and Uncle Buddy back in the 1920s.

Peanut Brittle

Along with hearth fires, this candy is a ritual of winter.

½ cup water
1 cup light corn syrup
2 cups sugar
Pinch of salt
2 cups peanuts
1 tablespoon baking soda
1 tablespoon butter
1 teaspoon vanilla

Place water, syrup, sugar, and salt in a medium saucepan and bring to a boil. Add peanuts, stirring occasionally to prevent sticking. Cook to 296°F on a candy thermometer. Remove from the heat and add baking soda, butter, and vanilla. Stir thoroughly. Pour onto a greased marble slab or greased baking pans. Spread quickly to ¼-inch thickness. When almost cold, loosen candy from slab with a spatula and break into small pieces.

Note: Vary your choice of nuts: brittle can be made with walnuts, pecans, or cashews. Use raw or roasted nuts.

CARAMELS

Another confection best made in cool weather.
Wrapping the pieces makes each piece a sweet gift.

100 CARAMELS

3 or 4 tablespoons butter, for buttering the pans
2 cups sugar
2 cups heavy cream, divided
1¾ cups light corn syrup
1 cup butter
1 teaspoon salt
1 teaspoon vanilla extract

Butter a 8 × 12-inch baking pan, for easier removal of foil; line with foil. Butter the foil. Butter a heavy 4-quart saucepan and combine sugar, 1 cup of the cream, corn syrup, butter, and salt. Cook, stirring with wooden spoon, over moderate heat for about 5 minutes, or until butter melts and sugar dissolves. *Do not* scrape down the sides of the pan. Continue cooking and stirring for 30 minutes, or until temperature reaches 242°F on a candy thermometer. Slowly add the remaining cup of cream while mixture continues to boil. Boil without stirring until temperature reaches 246°F, about 20 minutes. Remove pan from heat, add vanilla and stir just enough to blend. Pour mixture into prepared baking pan without scraping bottom of saucepan. Set pan on rack to cool. Cover with plastic wrap and let sit 4 hours or overnight in the refrigerator.

Turn pan upside down and peel off foil. Cut into 1-inch or smaller pieces with a sharp, heavy knife. Wrap each piece with squares of clear plastic wrap or foil. Caramel can be stored at room temperature for 1 week, or refrigerated for up to 2 weeks.

DIVINITY

Little clouds of sweetness.

1 ½ DOZEN CANDIES

2 cups sugar
½ cup light corn syrup
¼ teaspoon salt
½ cup hot water
2 egg whites
½ cup chopped pecans or walnuts, optional
2 teaspoons vanilla extract

In a medium saucepan, dissolve sugar, syrup, and salt in hot water. Cook over medium-high heat without stirring until temperature reaches 248°F. With a damp cloth, wash down any crystals that form on the side of the pan during cooking. With an electric mixer, beat the egg whites until stiff. Remove the sugar syrup from the heat and pour gradually over the stiffly beaten egg whites, beating constantly with a wire whisk. Add nuts, if desired. Add vanilla extract and continue beating until mixture will hold its shape when dropped from a spoon. Let candy sit for 10 to 15 minutes if it is not holding its shape. Drop by teaspoonfuls onto waxed paper on a cool surface. Candies should set up in 1 hour.

Note: If the divinity becomes too stiff to handle, add a few drops of hot water to bring it back to a manageable consistency.

Making Candy Dandy

Making candy on a humid day is a lesson in failure. On rainy days or in the summer, cook the syrup to 240°F instead of 238°F and it might set up beautifully . . . or it might not. Candy making, you might say, is an art, not a science. But it is best to make candy on cold, clear days. Don't despair if your first efforts at candy making flop. It takes fortitude and practice, but success will surely be yours.

One No Trump

The first child to wake up, I encountered the remains of the midnight bridge party: ashtrays, glasses half full, wooden bowls with roasted nuts, a platter with two glorious pieces of fudge remaining. Surely my parents must not have noticed there was any left. I had observed on occasion what fudge did to them. It lured them away from their everyday straight and narrow paths into naughtiness. They went on late into the night, laughing, dealing cards, and sipping drinks till the wee hours of the morning.

I took the plate, settled myself comfortably into the velvet chair, and savored bite by early morning bite the dark, moist, and dangerous chocolate.

Mother's Fudge

Known to cause serious cravings.

24 SQUARES

3 cups sugar
½ cup butter
1 cup whole milk
Dash of salt
4 ounces unsweetened chocolate
1 teaspoon vanilla extract
1 cup chopped pecans or walnuts

Butter an 8 × 8-inch pan. Combine sugar, butter, milk, salt, and chocolate in medium saucepan. Stirring constantly, cook over medium heat until all ingredients melt and come to a boil. *Do not* scrape down the sides of the pan. Lower heat, insert candy thermometer, and let boil slowly *without stirring* for about 10 minutes or until soft ball forms when dropped in a cup of cold water (238°F on a candy thermometer). Remove pan from heat and cool. Add vanilla. Beat steadily until fudge loses its gloss. Add nuts. Pour into pan. Cool for 20 minutes and cut into squares. Store in airtight container or wrap in tin foil.

Don't Fudge It!

The trick to perfect fudge is cooking the chocolate mixture to precisely the correct temperature. Undercooking creates fudge that is too soft and won't set up; overcooking will harden the fudge so that it won't come out of the cooking pan. A candy thermometer will eliminate any guesswork. Be sure to insert it at least two inches deep into the chocolate mixture.

CHOCOLATE-COVERED PEANUT BUTTER BONBONS

If you stay home from work to eat bonbons, these are the ones.

125 BONBONS

1 cup butter
2¾ cups powdered sugar
2½ cups graham cracker crumbs,
    crushed very fine
2 cans (3¼ ounces each) flaked coconut
One l-pound jar peanut butter
18 ounces semisweet chocolate chips
3 tablespoons shortening

Melt butter and blend with sugar and crumbs in a large bowl. Add coconut and peanut butter and blend with hands. Shape into tightly packed balls about the size of large marbles. In a double boiler, melt chocolate chips and shortening and heat through. (If you dip your candy in melted chocolate before it gets hot enough, too much chocolate will stay on candy.) Spear the balls with toothpicks and dip individually in chocolate mixture to coat. Place the balls on waxed paper. Allow to set at room temperature for at least an hour. Store candies, tightly covered, between layers of waxed paper in the refrigerator.

Note: This recipe makes a large quantity—a perfect gift-making project. Forming the balls is time-consuming, so I make these in 2 sessions. The peanut

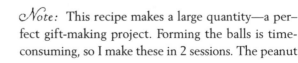

butter mixture and the chocolate can be refrigerated overnight. Let the peanut butter mixture come to room temperature when you resume, and reheat the chocolate in the double boiler.

CANDIED FRUIT PEELS DIPPED IN CHOCOLATE

As a child, these beauties were far too sophisticated for my young palate. Now, I love them and have added the chocolate dip.

48 CANDIES

3 medium to large navel oranges,
   bright skinned and unblemished
1½ cups water
1 cup sugar
3 tablespoons light corn syrup
½ cup sugar for rolling
18 ounces semisweet chocolate chips
3 tablespoons shortening

To candy the fruit, with a sharp knife cut a slice off the top and bottom of the oranges. Score the peel in four sections and pry the peel off. (You can also use a potato peeler.) Save the fruit for another use.

Scrape the white pith from inside the peel. Combine the peel in a heavy bottomed saucepan with enough water to float without being crowded. Bring to a boil and simmer for 10 minutes. Drain the water but leave the peel, add the same amount of fresh water and

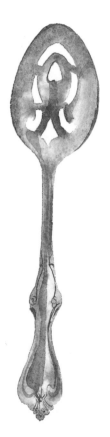

boil for another 10 minutes. Drain the water again, add fresh water, and cook the peel until it is tender, 15 to 25 minutes. Drain in a wire mesh sieve. Cool and cut the peel into slivers with a sharp knife or kitchen shears.

In the same saucepan, combine 1½ cups water with the sugar and corn syrup. Bring to a boil and boil for 3 minutes. Add the peel and cook, covered, until the peel looks translucent. Remove the cover and continue to cook until the syrup reduces to a spoonful or two. Watch carefully so that the peel doesn't burn. Fork onto a wire rack to cool. Coat a baking sheet with ½ cup sugar. While still warm, roll the peel in the sugar and let dry thoroughly at room temperature, about 2 hours.

In a double boiler, melt chocolate chips and shortening. Melt and heat through. (If you dip your candy in melted chocolate before it gets hot enough, too much chocolate will stay on candy.) Hold the peel by one end and dip into the chocolate halfway up the peel and place on waxed paper. Allow to set at room temperature for at least an hour. Store candies, tightly covered, between layers of waxed paper in a cool place.

Note: You can use oranges, grapefruits, or lemons, but cook them in separate batches.

Good Tempered

Tempering is the process of melting and cooling chocolate at precise temperatures so that it cools and then hardens with a smooth, glossy, and unstreaked finish. If you are reaching for perfection when dipping fruits or cookies, I recommend a three-step tempering method.

First, using sweetened or semisweet chocolate (block or chips), melt and then continue heating the chocolate until it reaches a temperature of 105°F to 110°F, which separates the cocoa butter from the chocolate mass. If not separated, the cocoa butter will not emulsify evenly when stirred, causing white streaks in the set chocolate. It is also possible that the chocolate might be grainy in texture and dull in appearance.

Next, cool the chocolate to about 75°F. This is necessary for emulsification, the thorough blending of the cocoa butter back into the chocolate mass. I add a tablespoon or two of grated chocolate to the pan to bring down the temperature more quickly.

Finally, reheat the chocolate to 92°F, which is the proper temperature for coating or dipping. The chocolate is now tempered and warm enough to coat smoothly. (If allowed to cool below 91°F, the coating will be too thick and dull rather than shiny.)

Once you have dipped your confections, the chocolates must be properly cooled. To retain the high gloss and firm texture, place the candies on a rack in a cool room with good air circulation (or in the refrigerator) until the chocolate has set. Allow them to warm to a moderate temperature of 65°F to 70°F. Store the candies uncovered at the same temperature for at least 24 hours before packaging.

Pralines

Emblematic of Southern hospitality: sugary sweet.

8 PRALINES

1 cup plus 1 tablespoon sugar
½ cup heavy cream
¼ teaspoon cream of tartar
Pinch of salt
1 cup pecan halves

Butter a heavy baking sheet. In a smooth, heavy skillet, combine the sugar, cream, and cream of tartar. Cook over medium heat, stirring occasionally until the sugar has completely melted and has turned a rich golden amber. As soon as the syrup has turned color, remove from the heat, add salt, and beat until creamy. Add the nuts. Pour into round wafers about 2 inches in diameter on baking sheet. Cool completely until set, about 1 hour.

Note: To make praline powder, put a few pralines into a food processor and grind until fine. Sprinkle as a topping for ice cream, puddings, or custards.

PULLED MINTS

These must be made on a cold, wintry day. Best to use children to help pull. These are creamy bites that melt in your mouth, and it is very difficult to stop eating them. A tin of them makes a charming gift.

3 DOZEN MINTS

2 tablespoons butter
½ cup water
2 cups sugar
6 to 7 drops peppermint extract
Food coloring, if desired

In a large saucepan, melt butter. Add water and sugar and stir over medium heat until dissolved. Cook to 260°F on candy thermometer or to the soft ball stage. (See Don't Fudge It, p. 53.) Pour immediately onto cool buttered marble slab or greased cookie sheet, add peppermint (and coloring), and as the edges cool, lift each edge once toward the center of the mass using a knife or spatula. Run your hands under cold water so that they will be cool, then dry and butter them. Pick up the hot candy as soon as it is possible to hold it and work quickly by yourself or with assistance from another person. Pull vigorously and evenly out from the center about 6 to 12 inches. Double it over and continue to pull in this way until the candy is stiff, hard to pull, and no longer glossy. Twist and form into a long rope about ½ inch in diameter, lay back out on the buttered slab and cut with kitchen shears into ½-inch pieces. Place pieces on waxed paper to finish cooling, about 30 minutes. When cool, pack in layers in airtight containers to "cream," or mellow and turn creamy. Set in a warm—not hot—place. They will cream in 24 hours.

Note: For creamy white mints, leave out food coloring completely.

SIMPLE BUTTER MINTS

Pam makes these at Christmas in the shape of bite-size trees.

3 TO 4 DOZEN MINTS

½ cup butter, at room temperature
3¾ cup confectioners' sugar
1 tablespoon heavy cream
6 to 7 drops peppermint extract
Food coloring, if desired

In a medium bowl, cream butter thoroughly; add sugar gradually and mix well. Add cream, peppermint, and coloring and blend. Spoon batter into a cake decorator tube, and using a shaped tip, press shapes onto waxed paper and let set up for 30 minutes. Store in an airtight container in a cool place.

Miss Trixie's Candied Popcorn

Belonging to the festive and fun category.
A cheery, afternoon treat.

2 GALLONS

1 cup popping corn
6 tablespoons vegetable oil
1 cup butter
2¼ cups light brown sugar
½ teaspoon salt
½ cup light corn syrup
¼ teaspoon cream of tartar
1 tablespoon vanilla
½ teaspoon baking soda

Preheat oven to 225°F.

To make 2 gallons of popcorn, pop the corn in a 4-quart popper in 2 batches, using ½ cup corn and 3 tablespoons oil for each batch. Place the popcorn in oven to keep warm.

In a large saucepan, melt butter. Add sugar, salt, and syrup. Stir until dissolved, and boil to bring the mixture to 245°F. Remove from heat and stir in cream of tartar, vanilla, and baking soda. Remove popcorn from the oven, add the hot syrup, and stir as quickly as possible until the popcorn is coated throughout. Put back in the oven and stir every 15 minutes for 1 hour. Remove from the oven. Spread out to cool on waxed paper. Store in an airtight container.

Rich

I knew when I grew up I would be as wealthy as Miss Ayres. She had everything that defined a proper lady of leisure. Her house sat proudly on Main Street in Danville, Virginia, surrounded by gardens filled with verbena and roses. I saw my reflection in her gold leaf pier mirror every time I entered her foyer, which was as big as our living room. Her down-filled couches were covered in velvet, and as I sank into them, I could imagine myself as the breathtakingly beautiful young girl in the painting above the mantle. Her chandeliers and lamps had the same kind of crystals Pollyanna used to make rainbows on the walls. Even the delicate opera creams her maid served with minted iced tea were creamier and more divine than they were when we made them at home.

OPERA CREAMS

I don't know what these have to do with opera. They are a maple-flavored version of fudge, but they can be a nutty vanilla-flavored version if you want to omit the maple flavor.

24 TO 36 PIECES

3 cups sugar
1 cup heavy cream
1 tablespoon corn syrup
4 tablespoons butter
¼ teaspoon salt
2 drops maple flavoring (not maple syrup)
2 teaspoons vanilla
1 cup pecans, sliced thin

Combine sugar, cream, corn syrup, butter, and salt in a heavy saucepan and cook over low heat until sugar is dissolved, stirring constantly. Cook to soft ball stage (238°F on candy thermometer), stirring occasionally. Remove from heat, and add maple flavoring and vanilla. Pour into a large bowl and beat with a mixer until creamy. Add pecans. Drop by teaspoonfuls onto buttered waxed paper. Let cool for 1 hour. Store in an airtight container between layers of waxed paper.

Cookies
&
Bars

Ten Hut

*M*ajor Allison's house loomed over Davie Avenue, gothic and authoritative. Allison, his grand-daughter and youngest of eight in the prominent family, was my best friend.

The house, surrounded by majestic live oaks and swarms of azaleas, stood four houses from Davie Avenue Elementary, and most every afternoon Allison and I ran there as soon as school let out. The center hallway of the house was always cool, and the back door to the garden was usually open, throwing light down the dark mahogany hall. Standing in the cool, dark hall, the bright rectangle of fuzzy green was like a perfect world just beyond my reach.

Major Allison was always seated in his book-lined study, hand on cane, and he'd bellow his customary greeting, "Come in, girls!" A generous tray awaited our arrival, filled with meringue surprises, chess chewies, scotchies, and milk.

He'd ask gruffly, yet politely, about our day. And then he'd tell us a story. We sat at his feet munching, transfixed, as he told a tale of another, more glorious South long before us.

CHESS CHEWIES

These are very sweet and gooey. Cold milk is the companion of choice.

24 TO 36 SQUARES

2¼ cups dark brown sugar
1 cup sugar
4 eggs
1½ teaspoons vanilla
1 cup butter, melted
2 cups all-purpose flour
2 teaspoons baking powder
¼ teaspoon salt
1 cup pecans, chopped

Preheat oven to 350°F.

In a large mixing bowl, combine sugars, eggs, vanilla, and melted butter and beat well. In a separate bowl, sift together flour, baking powder, and salt; add to sugar mixture. Fold in nuts. The batter will be very stiff. Spread the batter in a well-greased 13 × 9 × 2-inch pan. Bake in 350°F oven (or 325°F if using a Pyrex pan) for 30 to 40 minutes, until firm. Cool for 20 minutes; cut into bars or squares, but leave in the pan until completely cool.

ORANGE BLOSSOMS

These delectable little morsels are, admittedly, a whole lot of trouble and very time-consuming. But they're also unique, and even the most experienced bakers will have trouble guessing how they're made. Be careful; people eat them like peanuts.

6 DOZEN

Icing:

4 cups confectioners' sugar
1 tablespoon orange zest
1 cup freshly squeezed orange juice, strained
1 teaspoon lemon zest
½ cup freshly squeezed lemon juice, strained
Pinch of salt

Batter:

1 cup shortening
1½ cups sugar
1 teaspoon vanilla
2 eggs
2¼ cups sifted cake flour
1½ teaspoons baking powder
1 teaspoon salt
1 cup milk

Preheat oven to 350°F.

In a medium bowl, combine all of the icing ingredients and mix until smooth. Set aside.

In a medium bowl, cream shortening and sugar until very light and fluffy. Add vanilla and eggs and mix well. In a separate bowl, sift flour with baking powder and salt and add to creamed mixture alternately with milk. Cover with a damp cloth until ready to use.

Drop batter a teaspoonful at a time into each well of greased *mini* muffin tins. Bake in the oven for 8 to 10 minutes or until just lightly brown and set. Flip out with a thin spatula and drop into icing while still hot. Drain each cookie with a slotted spoon and place on waxed paper to cool. Can be refrigerated for 2 weeks or frozen with waxed paper between layers. Delicious at room temperature or chilled.

PAM'S FROSTY DATE BALLS

How could these possibly be so good and so simple to make? We always serve them at Christmas on a pedestal cake plate with our other favorite cookies.

3 DOZEN

½ cup butter
1 cup brown sugar
One 8-ounce package of dates, chopped
2 cups crisp rice cereal
½ cup pecans, chopped
½ cup shredded coconut
2 cups confectioners' sugar

In a medium saucepan, slowly heat butter, brown sugar, and dates until dates are completely incorporated. Remove from the heat and stir in cereal, nuts, and coconut. Let mixture cool enough to handle. Form into balls roughly 1 inch in diameter, and roll each ball in confectioners' sugar. Store in an airtight container at room temperature.

Gumdrop Cookies

Cutting the gumdrops is tedious, as they stick to the scissors, but children absolutely adore these colorful and festive Christmas cookies. There's no fat in these, but they aren't diet food either.

2 DOZEN COOKIES

2 tablespoons water
4 eggs
2 cups brown sugar
2 cups all-purpose flour
¼ teaspoon salt
1 teaspoon cinnamon
1 cup gumdrops, fruit flavors
   (not the spiced kind),
   cut in small pieces
¾ cup walnuts, finely chopped

Preheat oven to 325°F.

In medium bowl, mix water and eggs and beat until very fluffy, about 3 to 5 minutes. Add sugar and mix well. In a separate bowl, sift flour, salt, and cinnamon together; add to egg mixture and stir until well blended. Toss gumdrops in ¼ cup flour. Discard flour and add gumdrops and nuts to batter and blend well. Pour into greased 9 × 12-inch pan. Bake for 30 minutes, watching carefully to make sure batter is not browning too quickly. Let cool 10 minutes. Frost with Orange Butter Frosting. Cut into squares while warm. When cool, remove from pan and store in an airtight container.

Orange Butter Frosting

2 CUPS

3 tablespoons butter, softened
2 cups confectioners' sugar
2 tablespoons fresh orange juice
Grated rind of 1 orange

Combine all ingredients in a medium bowl and mix well. Spread over warm cookies.

MERINGUE SURPRISES

*Delicate and light, these sweets melt in your mouth.
You can replace the chocolate pieces with coconut
or nuts.*

2 DOZEN MERINGUES

2 egg whites
⅛ teaspoon salt
⅛ teaspoon cream of tartar
1 teaspoon vanilla
¾ cup sugar
1 cup semisweet chocolate pieces
¼ cup chopped walnuts, optional

Preheat oven to 300°F.

In a medium bowl, beat egg whites, salt, cream of tartar, and vanilla until soft peaks form. Add sugar gradually, beating until stiff peaks form. Fold in chocolate pieces and nuts. Cover cookie sheet with plain brown paper (we use brown paper grocery bags cut to fit the baking sheet) or baking parchment. Drop mixture by rounded teaspoonfuls onto sheet. Bake about 25 minutes until lightly brown. Cool slightly before removing from the paper. Store in an airtight container.

PECAN DROPS

Nary a drop will be left.

2 ½ TO 3 DOZEN COOKIES

½ cup butter
½ cup sugar plus ½ cup firmly packed dark brown sugar, *or* 1 cup light brown sugar
1 egg, beaten well
½ cup all-purpose flour
¼ teaspoon salt
1 teaspoon vanilla
1 cup chopped pecans

Preheat oven to 350°F.

In a medium bowl, cream butter and sugars until light and fluffy. Add egg, flour, and salt and mix well. Add vanilla and pecans and blend. Drop by teaspoonfuls onto greased cookie sheet and bake for 10 minutes or until lightly browned. Remove while still warm and cool on racks. Store in an airtight container.

Libby Robbins's Scotchies

*Libby Robbins is a gifted costume designer,
her husband a great violinist, and her daughter
a brilliant dancer. These are artist's cookies.*

2 DOZEN COOKIES

½ cup shortening
1 cup dark brown sugar
1 egg
1 teaspoon vanilla
1 cup all-purpose flour
½ teaspoon soda
½ teaspoon salt
1 cup quick-cook oats (not instant)
1 cup coconut
½ cup pecans or walnuts, chopped

Preheat oven to 325°F.

In a medium bowl, cream shortening and sugar. Beat
in egg and vanilla. In a separate bowl, sift flour, soda,
and salt. Add to egg mixture. Stir in oats, coconut,
and nuts. Drop by teaspoon onto greased cookie sheets
and flatten slightly with the palm of your hand. Bake
for 12 minutes or until brown. Remove from the
cookie sheet while warm. Let cool on racks.

Mrs. Whitmore's Cookies

No one knows who Mrs. Whitmore is, but her name has an authoritative ring to it. The recipe comes from my sister Pam's college roommate, who supplied these cookies to sustain long all-nighters.

36 SQUARES

1 cup sugar
1 cup butter
2 cups all-purpose flour
2 tablespoons vanilla
1 egg, separated
2 cups chopped pecans

Preheat oven to 325°F.

In a medium bowl, cream together sugar and butter. Add flour, vanilla, and egg yolk. The dough will be stiff. Press into an 11 × 15-inch jelly roll pan with your hands. Brush with lightly beaten egg white. Sprinkle pecans across dough, then press them into dough with your hands. Bake for 25 to 30 minutes. (The pecans may brown quickly and burn, so check often.) Let cool for 5 minutes and cut into squares. These cookies freeze well.

Hats On

Mrs. Ford sold hats for Spainhour's, Statesville's sole and family-run department store.

On my numerous after-school visits she allowed me to try on any hat in the millinery department. It was wonderful. Everywhere hats were posed on pedestals. Velvet-tufted chairs at dainty vanities awaited the customers with ivory-handled mirrors so that they could consider hats from the back. In 1964, Jackie O. pillboxes, brimmed numbers adorned with flowers, ribbons, tiers, and veils, were the hats of choice for the ladies who churched.

Mrs. Ford's cookies were no less inspired than her hats. In fact, her cookies often looked like her hats, or her hats looked like her cookies. In her tiny powder blue office she would pull out a tin that might contain Orange Blossoms in April, Lemon Kisses in July, or Pecan Drops in October. I was allowed to wear a hat as I ate her seasonal cookies at Spainhour's. She said it was a good way for me to rehearse having tea with the queen.

LEMON KISSES

There are many variations on lemon squares; I prefer mine very tangy and with a crisp bottom crust. Only fresh lemon juice should be used. Obviously, since I recommend the use of the food processor, this is not an old family recipe, but it quickly became a standard in the Southern repertoire of the early '70s.

4 DOZEN SQUARES

Crust:

1 cup softened butter
½ cup confectioners' sugar
2 cups all-purpose flour
Pinch of salt

Filling:

4 eggs
2 cups sugar
5 tablespoons all-purpose flour
Pinch of salt
6 tablespoons freshly squeezed lemon juice
1 to 2 tablespoons grated lemon rind

Glaze:

2 cups confectioners' sugar
1 tablespoon soft butter
Pinch of salt
3 tablespoons lemon juice

Preheat oven to 325°F.

For the crust, mix butter, sugar, flour, and salt in a food processor until blended. Pat evenly into the bottom of a lightly greased 13 × 9 × 2-inch pan. Bake for 15 to 20 minutes or until puffed and very lightly browned. Remove from the oven and turn the oven up to 350°F.

For the filling, in the same bowl, mix eggs and sugar together. In a separate bowl, sift flour and salt; add to egg mixture and mix well. Add lemon juice and rind. Pour over crust; bake 15 to 20 minutes at 350°F. Remove from the oven.

For the glaze, combine confectioners' sugar, butter, salt, and lemon juice in a processor bowl. Spread evenly over filling. Cool. Cut into 3-inch squares.

Note: The bowl of the processor does not need to be washed between crust and topping, only rinsed before making the glaze. Or you may omit the glaze and sift confectioners' sugar over the top. I prefer a glaze to confectioners' sugar, but both are tasty.

Favorite Cakes

Spirit Willing, Flesh Weak

When Mother gave me a jar of her fig preserves, she must have been feeling mighty generous. She suffered a wasp sting while picking a paltry crop and only got seven jars from the Brown Turkey fig tree after the April frost wiped out most of the buds. Dan Perry would sometimes bring her some of his coveted crop from Hatteras where figs are considered an island treasure, guarded and nurtured like sacred cows. My one jar containing golden orbs of sweetness like no other, with just the thinnest sliver of lemon peel, was eaten before it was ever used in a cake.

SYLLABUB

A very old and favorite recipe, dating back to the eighteenth century. Served in goblets it is elegant and spirited.

4 SERVINGS

¼ cup white wine or dry sherry
2 tablespoons brandy
Juice of 1 lemon
Pared rind of lemon, reserving
    ¼ of the rind for garnish
4 tablespoons sugar
½ pint of heavy cream
Dash of nutmeg

Mix white wine, brandy, lemon juice, and rind together in a small bowl, cover, and refrigerate overnight. Strain the liquid into a bowl and add the sugar, stirring until it dissolves. Whip the cream until it just holds its shape in soft peaks. Add nutmeg. Stir the wine mixture slowly into the whipped cream. Spoon gently into small glasses and chill before serving.

Blanch the reserved lemon rind gently in boiling water for 15 minutes, drain and cool. Place a cluster of rind on top of each serving.

Note: Can be made a day in advance of serving. A chardonnay is a nice choice for the wine.

Embellishments

Raspberry Sauce

A burst of summer for winter desserts. Serve with November Pudding (p. 37) or Warm Chocolate Cake (p. 95).

2 CUPS

2 cups fresh raspberries, washed and drained,
    without syrup or juice
2 tablespoons sugar
1 teaspoon kirsch, Grand Marnier, or cognac
1 tablespoon lemon juice

Puree all ingredients in a food processor or blender until smooth. Chill for at least 1 hour.

Note: If using frozen berries, allow them to defrost.

Bourbon Sauce

Serve with November Pudding (p. 37), Wild Persimmon Pudding (p. 32), or Apricot Bread Pudding (p. 39). Sure to add sparkle.

1 CUP

1 cup heavy cream
½ vanilla bean, split lengthwise
3 egg yolks
⅓ cup sugar
3 tablespoons bourbon

In a medium saucepan, combine the heavy cream and the vanilla bean. Bring just to a boil. Pour the cream into a bowl, leaving the vanilla bean in the hot cream for about 10 minutes. Remove the bean and scrape any pulp into the cream. Discard the bean.

Beat together the egg yolks and sugar. Stir ½ cup of the hot cream into the egg yolks, stirring constantly. Pour back into the saucepan along with the remaining cream. Stir and cook over low heat about 3 minutes or until bubbly, then stir and cook 2 minutes more. Remove from the heat and stir in the bourbon. Strain and serve warm.

Hot Fudge Sauce

This ubiquitous and versatile sauce is essential for ice cream and Cream Puffs (p. 98), and even adds to leftover vanilla puddings and custards.

2 CUPS

7 ounces bittersweet chocolate
¼ cup sugar
½ cup light corn syrup
½ cup plus 1 tablespoon water
¾ cup unsweetened cocoa powder
½ cup brewed coffee
3 tablespoons cognac or brandy

Cut chocolate into 2-inch pieces. In a double boiler, melt chocolate over barely simmering water. Remove the double boiler from the heat and let the chocolate stand over warm water until ready to use.

I like ingredients for my desserts to be as good and as fresh as they can possibly be so that the finished product will be intensely flavored. When it comes to chocolate, I'm choosy, but I have always been very happy with the results of baking with domestic chocolate. My absolute favorite is Nestlé's.

Combine the sugar, corn syrup, water, cocoa powder, and coffee in a large saucepan and bring to a boil. Boil for 1 to 2 minutes, stirring constantly to prevent burning on the bottom. When the surface is covered with bubbles, remove from the heat and whisk in the warm chocolate. Return to the heat and let boil for a few minutes to reduce until the mixture is as thick as you like. Stir in the spirits.

Let cool slightly before using. Stored in the refrigerator, the sauce lasts indefinitely. Reheat in a bowl over simmering water.

REAL WHIPPED CREAM

It's best to make whipped cream right before serving; it must be kept refrigerated and cannot sit at room temperature for longer than 20 to 30 minutes. The butter adds texture and body to plain whipped cream, and resembles old-timey heavy cream. You need only serve a small dollop.

1 ½ CUPS

1 cup heavy cream
¼ cup butter, softened
1 teaspoon vanilla
2 tablespoons confectioners' sugar

Chill bowl and beaters. Heat ¼ cup of heavy cream slowly in a saucepan; add butter, stirring until butter is just melted. Cool to room temperature. Add vanilla and reserve.

In chilled bowl, beat remaining ¾ cup cream and sugar until thick. Add butter mixture with beater on low and then beat until stiff peaks form.

AUNT LEECIE'S CUSTARD SAUCE

3 CUPS

6 egg yolks, lightly beaten
⅔ cup sugar
Pinch of salt
2 cups half-and-half, at room temperature
1 teaspoon vanilla or 2 tablespoons bourbon

In bottom of double boiler, bring one inch of water (water must not touch top of pan) to simmer over medium heat. In the top of a double boiler, beat together egg yolks, sugar, and salt until thick and light-colored. Gradually add half-and-half. Heat, stirring constantly until mixture is somewhat thickened and coats a spoon. Mixture must not come to a boil or it will curdle. Remove from heat and add vanilla or bourbon. Chill.

This is one from the handwritten recipe book of Aunt Leecie in Nevada, Missouri. Luscious on the fruits of summer, particularly under the stars with the grown-ups singing "There's a Long, Long Trail" or "Mighty Like a Rose."

NORMAN'S NOG

This was a much beloved beverage of Christmas, either for the grown-ups early Christmas morning (fortified with bourbon), or late in the day after dinner had a chance to settle. You'll need a large kettle for this, plus room in the refrigerator, or the back porch if it's cold enough, to store it.

8 SERVINGS

8 cups milk, heated until
    steaming
6 egg yolks
1 cup sugar
2 tablespoons cornstarch
¼ teaspoon salt
1 teaspoon vanilla

In a large saucepan, heat the milk, but do not boil. In a medium bowl, beat egg yolks, sugar, cornstarch, and salt until thick. Stir small amount, ½ cup, hot milk into egg mixture and mix well; add back to remaining hot mixture and cook until it coats the back of a spoon. (It won't be very thick but will thicken as it cools.) Add vanilla. Chill 2 hours before serving and flavor individually with bourbon to taste.

Index

A

ambrosia, 106–107
apple(s):
    cake, Pam's persimmon-, 96
    crisp, 14
    pears in nightshirts, 44–45
apricot bread pudding, 39
Aunt Leecie's custard sauce, 7, 119

B

baking tips, viii–ix
banana pudding, 34–35
bars and cookies, *see* cookies and
    bars
berries:
    blackberries bramble crumble, 13
    raspberry(ies):
        November pudding, 37–38
        sauce, 116
        summer pudding, 36–37
blackberries bramble crumble, 13
blind baking, 4
bonbons, chocolate-covered peanut
    butter, 54–55
bourbon:
    custard sauce, Aunt Leecie's, 7, 119
    sauce, 116–17
bramble crumble, 13
brandy:
    custard sauce, 110
    hot fudge sauce, 117–18
    syllabub, 113

bread pudding, apricot, 39
burnt-sugar cake with burnt-sugar
    frosting, 88–89
buttermilk:
    glaze, 82
    pie, 5

C

cakes, 80–99
    burnt-sugar, with burnt-sugar
        frosting, 88–89
    chocolate, warm, 95
    cream puffs, 98
    fig, 81–82
        buttermilk glaze for, 82
        fig preserves for, 83
    jelly roll, 85–86
    orange, Christmas, 90–91
    persimmon-apple, Pam's, 96
    pound cake with sherry sauce,
        sugar-crust, 92–93
candy, 48–63
    bonbons, chocolate-covered peanut
        butter, 54–55
    caramels, 50
    chocolate:
        candied fruit peels dipped in,
            55–56
        -covered peanut butter bonbons,
            54–55
    divinity, 51

fudge:
    candy thermometer used in
        making, 52
    Mother's, 53
    mints:
        pulled, 59
        simple butter, 60
    opera creams, 63
    peanut brittle, 49
    popcorn, Miss Trixie's candied, 61
    pralines, 58
    thermometer, 52
    weather conditions for making, 51
caramels, 50
caramelizing sugar toppings, torches
    for, 8
cherry pudding, Mom's, 31
chess pie, 6
    chocolate, 7
    lemon, Muzz's, 9
chocolate, 117
    cake, warm, 95
    candied fruit peels dipped in,
        55–56
    chess pie, 7
    -covered peanut butter bon-
    bons, 54–55
    fudge, Mother's, 53
    hot fudge sauce, 117–18
    meringue surprises, 71–72
    moon pie, 27
    pudding, 41
    tempering, 57

Christmas orange cake, 90–91
classic Southern pecan pie, 11
coconut:
    ambrosia, 106–107
    custard pie, 19
    date balls, Pam's frosty, 69
    scotchies, Libby Robbins's, 73
cognac:
    hot fudge sauce, 117–18
    raspberry sauce, 116
compote, frozen fruit, 105–106
cookies and bars, 66–77
    chess chews, 67
    date balls, Pam's frosty, 69
    frosting, orange butter, 71

cookies and bars *(continued)*:
  gumdrop, 70–71
  lemon kisses, 76–77
  meringue surprises, 71–72
  Mrs. Whitmore's, 74
  orange blossoms, 68–69
  pecan drops, 72
  scotchies, Libby Robbins's, 73
cream:
  bourbon sauce, 116–17
  ice cream, peach, 103–104
  opera creams, 63
  syllabub, 113
  whipped, real, 118–19
cream puffs, 98
crisps, 14
  apple, 14
crumbles, 14
  bramble, 13
crunches, 14
custard:
  pie, coconut, 19
  sauce, 110
  sauce, Aunt Leecie's, 7, 119
  vanilla, 99

D

date balls, Pam's frosty, 69

E

eggs:
  bourbon sauce, 116–17
  cream puffs, 98
  custard:
    pie, coconut, 19
    sauce, 110
    sauce, Aunt Leecie's, 7, 119
    vanilla, 99
  lemon meringue pie, 24–25
  meringue surprises, 71–72
  nog, Norman's, 120
  pound cake with sherry sauce, sugar-
    crust, 92–93
  pudding:
    banana, 34–35
    chocolate, 41
    November, 37–38
    raspberry summer, 36–37

F

figs:
  cake, 81–82
    buttermilk glaze for, 82
    fig preserves for, 83
  in spiced wine, 112
fried fruit pies, 15–16, 17–18
frosting:
  burnt-sugar, 89

orange butter, 71

frozen fruit compote, 105–106

fruit:

    ambrosia, 106–107

    compote, frozen, 105–106

    pies, fried, 15–16, 17–18

    see also specific fruits

fudge:

    candy thermometer used in making,
        53

    Mother's, 53

G

glazes:

    buttermilk, for fig cake, 82

    for Christmas orange cake, 91

graham cracker crust, 22

Grand Marnier:

    ambrosia, 106–107

    raspberry sauce, 116

gumdrop cookies, 70–71

H

hot fudge sauce, 117–18

I

ice cream:

    peach, 103–104

    snow cream, 104

J

jelly:

    roll, 85–86

    wine, 109

K

Kay Bennett's deep-dish sweet potato
    pudding, 42–43

L

lemon:

    chess pie, Muzz's, 9

    kisses, 76–77

    meringue pie, 24–25

    syllabub, 113

Libby Robbins's scotchies, 73

M

meringue surprises, 71–72

mints:

    pulled, 59

    simple butter, 60

Miss Trixie's candied popcorn, 61

Mom's cherry pudding, 31

moon pie, 27

Mother's fudge, 53

Mrs. Whitmore's cookies, 74

Muzz's lemon chess pie, 9

N

Norman's nog, 120
November pudding, 37–38
nuts, *see specific types of nuts*

O

oats:
    scotchies, Libby Robbins's, 73
opera creams, 63
orange(s):
    ambrosia, 106–107
    butter frosting, 71
    cake, Christmas, 90–91
    candied fruit peels dipped in
      chocolate, 55–56
    orange blossoms (cookies),
      68–69

P

Pam's frosty date balls, 69
peace pie, 12
peach(es):
    ice cream, 103–104
    pie, peace, 12
    poached, with whole peppercorns, 111
peanut brittle, 49
peanut butter bonbons, chocolate-
    covered, 54–55
pears in nightshirts, 44–45
pecans:
    chess chews, 67

date balls, Pam's frosty, 69
drops, 72
fudge, Mother's, 53
Mrs. Whitmore's cookies, 74
opera creams, 63
pie, classic southern, 11
pralines, 58
sweet potato pudding, Kay Bennett's
    deep-dish, 42–43
peppercorns, poached peaches with
    whole, 111
persimmons, 33
    -apple cake, Pam's, 96
    pudding, wild, 32–33

pie(s), 3–27
  buttermilk, 5
  chess, 6
    chocolate, 7
    lemon, Muzz's, 9
  chocolate:
    chess, 7
    moon, 27
  coconut custard, 19
  fried fruit, 15–16, 17–18
  graham cracker crust, 22
  lemon:
    chess, Muzz's, 9
    meringue, 24–25
  moon, 27
  peace, 12
  pecan, classic southern, 11
  pumpkin chiffon, 21–22
  shell, 3–4
  shoofly, 23
  sugar, 4
poached peaches with whole
  peppercorns, 111
popcorn, Miss Trixie's candied, 61
pound cake with sherry sauce, sugar-
  crust, 92–93
pralines, 58
preserves, fig, 83
puddings:
  apricot bread, 39
  banana, 34–35
  cherry, Mom's, 31
  chocolate, 41

  November, 37–38
  raspberry summer, 36–37
  sweet potato, Kay Bennett's
    deep-dish, 42–43
  wild persimmon, 32–33
pulled mints, 59
pumpkin chiffon pie, 21–22

R

raspberry(ies):
  November pudding, 37–38
  sauce, 116
  summer pudding, 36–37
real whipped cream, 118–19
rice cereal:
  date balls, Pam's frosty, 69

S

sauce:
  bourbon, 116–17
  custard, 110
  custard, Aunt Leecie's, 7, 119
  hot fudge, 117–18
  raspberry, 116
  sherry, sugar-crust pound cake with,
    92–93
scotchies, Libby Robbins's, 73
sherry:
  custard sauce, 110
  sauce, sugar-crust pound cake with,
    92–93
  syllabub, 113
shoofly pie, 23

simple butter mints, 60

snow cream, 104

sugar:

    burnt-sugar cake with burnt-sugar
        frosting, 88–89

    for candy, *see* candy

    caramelizing, torch for, 8

    -crust pound cake with sherry sauce,
        92–93

    pie, 4

    vanilla, 36

sweet potato pudding, Kay Bennett's
    deep-dish, 42–43

syllabub, 113

T

tempering, 57

thermometer, candy, 52

torches for caramelizing sugar topping, 8

V

vanilla:

    custard, 99

    sugar, 36

W

walnuts:

    fudge, Mother's, 53

    gumdrop cookies, 70–71

    meringue surprises, 71–72

    scotchies, Libby Robbins's, 73

warm chocolate cake, 95

whipped cream, real, 118–19

wine:

    figs in spiced, 112

    jelly, 109

    syllabub, 113